jobsearch.net

Carrie Straub, MBA

Crisp Publications
Menlo Park, CA

jobsearch.net

Carrie Straub, MBA

CREDITS
Managing Editor: **Kathleen Barcos**
Editor: **Amy Marks**
Production: **Barbara Atmore**
Typesetting: **ExecuStaff**
Cover Design: **Fifth Street Design**

Copyright © 1998 by Crisp Publications, Inc.
Printed in the United States of America by Bawden Printing Company.
http://www.crisp-pub.com

Distribution to the U.S. Trade:

National Book Network, Inc.
4720 Boston Way
Lanham, MD 20706
1-800-462-6420

Library of Congress Catalog Card Number 97-77659
Straub, Carrie
jobsearch.net
ISBN 1-56052-451-0

This book is printed on recyclable paper with soy ink.

10 9 8 7 6 5 4 3 2 1

Acknowledgements

To my morale-boosting, resource-sharing, creative-conversation-holding and applause-giving colleagues and friends at the Washington State Department of Personnel Career Transistion Center; you have no equals.

To MaryLou Webb, author and Dean of the Institute for Management and Professional Development at Portland Community College, who is a model to all the many lives she touches.

To jobsearch.net readers:

I've made every effort to ensure that the URL's mentioned in this book are correct by visiting each of them and doing last-minute updates. However, the Internet changes rapidly, so don't be surprised if some have moved or disappeared when you try to find the address. Get in the habit of using a search engine to find the resources that interest you, bookmark your personal list and share the new things you found with someone you know.

My e-mail address is included. Let me know about your successes!

Happy and Successful Hunting!

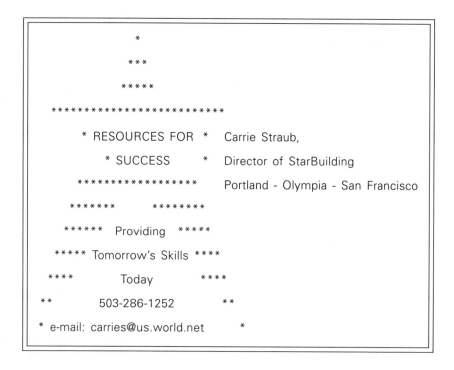

```
              *
            * * *
          * * * * *
* * * * * * * * * * * * * * * * * * * * * * * * *
      * RESOURCES FOR  *   Carrie Straub,
        * SUCCESS      *   Director of StarBuilding
      * * * * * * * * * * * * * *   Portland - Olympia - San Francisco
      * * * * * * *      * * * * * * *
      * * * * * *  Providing  * * * * *
      * * * * * Tomorrow's Skills * * * *
    * * * *        Today        * * * *
  * *          503-286-1252          * *
  * e-mail: carries@us.world.net      *
```

Contents

Introduction

Whether you are changing jobs, changing careers or just exploring your options—it doesn't matter if this is by choice or
necessity—imagine that the sky's the limit. In today's economy,
if you are competing for a job, a professional opportunity or a
project, you will need strategies for implementing traditional
job search activities quickly and effectively. If you are:

- Networking to find out about jobs
- Researching employers
- Getting your resume into employers' hands
- Finding education and gaining new skills
- Communicating with employers, colleagues or mentors

*The Internet expands your reach beyond
your wildest imagination.*

This book can help you in three key areas:

1. Changing the way you think about job searching and
   career planning
2. Getting you on-line and using the Internet in your job
   transition (what we'll call cybersearching)
3. Offering you specific on-line resources

1

This book is primarily about marketing a very special product—you! Designed to support you while you look for opportunities and present your experience in the marketplace of the next millennium, it mixes strategic marketing skills with electronic tools. It gives you practical, down-to-earth information about using the Internet in your job search, answering questions such as:

- What decisions must you make to get started?
- Who and what's out there?
- What tools will you need for an effective on-line job search?
- What does it mean to market yourself?
- How do you write a resume suitable for an on-line job search?
- What are key words and how do you decide which ones to use?
- What is the best style for Internet communication?
- What are the essentials of Netiquette?

Before you begin, you need to decide how comfortable you are with conducting a job search in general and how comfortable you are using electronic resources to conduct that search. The following readiness assessment will help you determine the best place to begin your search.

 ### *Exercise: Job Search Readiness Assessment*

1. How confident do you feel about your ability to develop a career plan and marketing strategy?

Not Confident   **Very Confident**

1   2   3   4   5

2. How ready are you to seek employment opportunities using nontraditional methods?

   Not Prepared   **Very Prepared**

   1   2   3   4   5

3. How confident do you feel about your ability to manage a successful job search?

   Not Confident   **Very Confident**

   1   2   3   4   5

4. How confident are you about using electronic tools for communication and research to support your job search?

   Not Confident   **Very Confident**

   1   2   3   4   5

5. If you have an updated resume, how confident are you that it will produce the results you desire?

   Not Confident   **Very Confident**

   1   2   3   4   5

6. How confident are you about the ability of your resume to represent you in the electronic marketplace?

   Not Confident   **Very Confident**

   1   2   3   4   5

7. How confident are you in your ability to draft a cover letter that will bring your resume to the attention of a prospective employer?

   Not Confident   **Very Confident**

   1   2   3   4   5

8. How confident are you about your ability to update your knowledge and skills with nontraditional sources?

   Not Confident   **Very Confident**

   1   2   3   4   5

9. How confident are you about translating your skills and experience into accomplishments or results?

   Not Confident   **Very Confident**

   1   2   3   4   5

10. How confident are you about transferring your experience to other industries?

    Not Confident   **Very Confident**

    1   2   3   4   5

11. How familiar are you with using electronic communication to network with friends and associates?

    Not Familiar   **Very Skilled**

    1   2   3   4   5

12. How much research time have you spent finding out about industries or organizations where you might apply?

    Very Little   **More Than Six Hours**

    1   2   3   4   5

NOTE: If you gave yourself a "3 or below" on the following items, you may want to try out these resources:

5: *Strategic Resumes* by Marci Mahoney, published by Crisp Publications, 1992.
7: http://www.adm.uwaterloo.ca:80/infocecs/CRC/manual/letters.html
10: *Finding Your Perfect Work* by Paul and Sarah Edwards.
11: http://www.paradesa.com, select "Learn the Net" and visit the e-mail lesson.

13. In what ways have you learned about job leads (check all that apply)?

☐ Newspaper ads   ☐ Friends or associates

☐ Business journal articles   ☐ Professional associations

☐ Internal job postings   ☐ Search firms

☐ Professional journal ads   ☐ Temporary agency placements

☐ Marketing letter sent to industry contacts   ☐ Referral from boss or supervisor

☐ "Grapevine": vendors, customers and so on

14. List three key factors that are motivating you to examine your career or start a job search.

_____

_____

_____

15. What items belong on your job search to-do list?

_____   _____

_____   _____

_____   _____

_____   _____

Using This Book Effectively

You can increase your return on investment from this book by identifying specific sections and resources appropriate to your own situation. You probably want to locate the many resources, information and ideas available. For you to do that most effectively, you need to have basic knowledge about computers and Internet tools. Refer to Appendix A if you aren't already familiar with how the Internet works or if you want a refresher. Appendix B contains a glossary of Internet terms. If, as you work through this book, you encounter terms that are new to you, take a look at these appendixes. Chances are, all the background information you need will be there. Use the chart below to determine which sections of this book will be most helpful to you. The recommendations below offer quick access to the topics that will give you the most for the time you invest.

If you . . .	Read These Sections	Be sure to . . .
Are a novice computer user and not familiar with the Internet	Appendix A, part 1	■ Use the bibliography for additional resources ■ Contact your local library or community college to find out about hands-on workshops ■ Do all the exercises
Are knowledgeable about computer operation, but unfamiliar with the Internet	Appendix A, part 2	■ Plan to spend time practicing with your browser ■ Visit the sites recommended for learning about searching for information on the Internet
Are familiar with computers and are proficient with a browser	Appendix A, part 3 or dive right in with Sections 1 through 4 (see page 7)	■ Scan the entire book and do the personal marketing exercises ■ Plan to spend time surfing and exploring the sites suggested ■ Develop your resume for electronic presentation

Now think about whether you need to lay some groundwork for your search, in clarifying your goals and objectives and identifying how best to meet them. You may be looking for guidance on developing personal marketing strategies for your job search. You may already know exactly what you want to do and are simply looking for some tips on using electronic resources to find a job.

If you . . .	Read These Sections	Be sure to . . .
Need to develop personal marketing strategies	Sections 1 and 2	■ Review the bibliography for resources ■ Use *Creating Your Skills Portfolio* by Carrie Straub as a reference for developing your electronic portfolio ■ Do all the exercises
Need to know how to market yourself on line	Sections 3 and 4	■ Use *Strategic Resumes* by Marci Mahoney to guide you as you develop your resume ■ Practice using on-line forms at the locations mentioned in Section 3 ■ Review electronic resources in Section 4
Need to know what resources are available for your on-line job search	Section 4	■ Review electronic resources in Section 4

HOW CAN YOU USE THE INTERNET IN YOUR SEARCH?

Think of Internet activity as a dynamic process of information movement. You can send and retrieve information at any hour, to or from any place that has an Internet address. The information can be in the form of text, graphics, music, even voices or videos. You can check out employers; research cities, states and regions; keep an eye peeled for opportunities; and get more information than you ever imagined. You can look at new products, check out job descriptions and company benefits or look at weather information for an area where jobs are open. You can create your own home page to show prospective employers a copy of your report to your division manager, a photo of you spot welding or the audio of your original piano composition.

INTERNET SURVEY '97
(CommerceNet/Nielsen Internet Demographics Survey 10/30/97)

Total persons with access to the World Wide Web: 51 million over age 16

Average use: 5.5 hours per week

Available at work: 54%

Available at home: 62%

Composition of users:
  66% are male
  25% have income greater than $80,000
  64% have at least a college degree
  14% (2.5 million) have purchased products over the Internet
  65% use the Internet for e-mail

Most common business uses:
  1. Gather information
  2. Collaborate with others
  3. Research competitors

Predictions from those in the know—recruiters and hiring managers—stress that as the on-line revolution continues to expand, job seekers will have access to a wider variety of positions through a growing number of international databases. Since these databases are easy to access and yield real results, on-line job listings are already replacing national newspaper and magazine classified ads. With expanded geographic boundaries for their job searches, people will increase their chances of getting new jobs more quickly. And on-line job postings aren't just for computer engineers and techies. A five-minute search using the Internet can turn up jobs for writers, artists, cooks, manufacturing technicians, or even CEOs of sporting goods manufacturing companies. About 60% of the approximately one million on-line job listings at any given time are for non-technical positions.

All the traditional career support activities, from assessing personal skills, to obtaining educational degrees, to receiving career coaching and help developing a resume, can be done on-line, harnessing the powerful tools available on the Internet. When you complete this book, you will have new tools for:

- Networking
- Finding job databases
- Researching employer listings and information
- Reading career magazines
- Getting career coaching
- Discovering educational opportunities
- Posting your resume
- Establishing your e-mail presence (which equals status in this emerging world)
- Creating electronic business cards

Who and What Is Out There?

Kids, scientists, banks, Fortune 500 companies, employers, job seekers and trainers from Australia to Zimbabwe . . .

Business relies heavily on communication. The Internet is changing the marketplace far more rapidly than did mass production or electricity. For the first time, employees can work in different parts of the world and still communicate quickly and cheaply. The centralized workplace, where each worker has a station or desk on site, is often one of the first things to go when expense-cutting measures are put into place. Virtual businesses are springing up that offer a new set of possibilities. Products are rushed to market, and global sales and purchases are possible for small companies. It's now an advantage to be small and responsive instead of big and bureaucratic. Many government agencies are on line with access for everyone.

Customers don't know (or care) where the workers are as long as high-quality products are delivered and maintained. Yesterday, if your car broke down in "Chaise Lounge, North Dakota," it could take days to locate a part to fix it. Today, electronic locator software allows the new part to be on its way in minutes.

Lifelong learning is the rule, not the exception. Classes, degree programs and discussion groups are available at a keystroke. Employees are expected to invest in learning new skills, staying with the same job for five years or less. The "one job" employee is nearly extinct in today's workplace.

Since at the click of a mouse you can contact people, government, large and small companies, research databases, schools, and professional associations, you may face the happy challenge of narrowing the field based on your decision criteria. The amount of time you can spend surfing in cyberspace is literally limited to the length of time you can stand to stay on the computer. For the career-minded, here are examples of places you can visit to get a taste of who's who on the Internet:

What's the Flip Side of the Web?

Although much of the excitement about the Internet and the Web is justified, the information superhighway has some speed bumps. Here are some challenges you need to be prepared for:

- The lack of control over the Internet is great for freedom of speech. This very fact means there is also great possibility for inaccurate and biased information to be spread as "truth."

- You may find the Web extremely slow to use or have trouble understanding how to use the long, sometimes complicated addresses that are needed for Web navigation.

- Privacy issues abound. Your e-mail address can be collected automatically by the sites you visit, and you may receive unsolicited e-mails. This is considered a serious breach of Netiquette. It still happens.

- Although "mass mailing" to employers is possible, it still takes work to collect and enter all the addresses for the employers you want to contact.

- When posting your resume on the Web, it is extremely important to have a marketing tool that represents you well. A poor state-of-the-art resume is still a poor resume. See Section 3 for guidelines on creating a resume suitable for an on-line job search.

- Learning to navigate the Internet takes some time and energy. Plan to make it a priority.

Government. Read the day-to-day doings of the Legislature, the U.S. House of Representatives is *http://www.house.gov,* and the U.S. Senate is *http://www.senate.gov.* Get employment figures from the Department of Labor at *http://www.dol.gov,* and population trends from the Census bureau at *http://www.census.gov.* Or you can e-mail the president at *president@whitehouse.gov.*

Industry. Coca-Cola, Intel, bed and breakfasts in New Jersey, auto parts and repair stores, as well as sales to purchasing to customer service to human resources departments of large and small companies. On the Web, visit *http://www.joeboxer.com* or *http://www.intel.com.*

Banking, retail stores and catalogs. Flowers, clothing, sporting goods and automobiles are all available on the Internet. Sales of goods on the Internet are expected to rise to $46 billion by 1998! For help with your finances, check out *http://www.qfn.com.*

Schools and colleges. In addition to developing many of the basic tools that form the Internet, more schools and colleges are now delivering education by the Internet. Colleges and universities were among the first to post listings of their open positions on the Internet. Visit the University of Phoenix at *http://www.uophx.edu/online.*

Employment services. State employment services and headhunter firms sponsor sites on the Internet. Many of these sites offer interest tests, resume-posting features and other career resources.

Cities, states and maps. If you want to get information about driver's license requirements or public transportation systems in Moscow, Paris, Rome, New York, Seattle, Vail or hundreds of other cities across the globe, it's all available. Many of these sites have jobs posted along with application forms right there on the Internet. Go to *http://www.yahoo.com* and select a city or state from the directory presented.

Special interest discussion groups. Cats, dogs, politics, cartoons, medical research, even store coupons and other "freebies." Visit the FREE Forum at *http://www.FREEforum.com/* for ways to save money. Also try *http://www.webwiz.com/freeweb/access.htm* for a listing of free web services.

Libraries, museums, history and arts. You can visit the Smithsonian, take the kids to the Children's Museum in Seattle and listen to music or view paintings in the Louvre. Try *http://www.elibrary.com*.

Before you explore a particular on-line resource, you should think about what you hope to get from the resource. Review the following questions and develop an answer to each:

- Why am I exploring this resource?
- Will I be willing to relocate if I find a dream job on the other side of the state? The country? The world?
- What are my constraints? How will I make decisions about possible opportunities?
- What effort am I willing to invest in research to assist me in decisions about the career path I want to pursue?
- Am I goal-oriented and self-disciplined? For example, if I decide to get my education at an on-line university, do I have the drive to carry it out?
- Am I change oriented? Or change resistant? Do I welcome new challenges?

- How far do I want to "push the envelope"? Will I want to build my own Web page? Informational interview with an IRC? Post my resume? Answer job postings?

- Do I want to learn to use the Internet as a tool or as a creative opportunity?

Clearly these questions have no right or wrong answers. For better or worse, there are only *your* answers. Let your gut reaction guide you as you develop your marketing plan.

 ### Exercise: What Will This Mean to the Job Seeker?

Take a few minutes to compare the 1980s workplace to the future based on the implications of Internet communication. Consider the changes in these areas today, as opposed to 10 or 15 years ago, then add others that occur to you.

Changes in the skills needed to do the job:

_____

_____

_____

_____

Changes in the way employers hire employees:

_____

_____

_____

_____

Changes in the way products are purchased:

_____

_____

_____

_____

Changes in the way managers communicate with their workers:

_____

_____

_____

_____

Changes in the workplace:

_____

_____

_____

_____

Other changes, for example, in lifestyles, cultures, relationships:

_____

_____

_____

_____

Summarize the lists above by completing the following sentence:
*To be more effective in job searching, given the global electronic
communication capabilities I now have, I will need to:*

_____

_____

_____

_____

Top Skills for Today's Employment	
Skill	% of Occupations Requiring Skill
Use computer keyboard	40%
Use word-processing software	25%
Understand operating manuals	35%
What do you have to market in these areas?	

Benefits of Cybersearching

Surveys suggest that cybersearching reduces time from job
vacancy to hire, reduces expenses and shows the candidate's
skills and accomplishments more readily.

As a candidate for a job, a career changer or a retiree with an
interest in a different job, this may be a new experience, one
that requires you to change your thinking from local to global,
moving from verbal to visual (though your writing skills will
be more important than ever) and acting in minutes instead
of days.

On the other hand, using e-mail to submit your resume saves
postage, paper and time. The Internet lets you contact more
employers in a more targeted way. You can use the Internet to

get the real scoop on employers, bone up on mission statements, read product releases and press statements. You'll even be able to read job descriptions, complete applications on-line and find out about employee benefits. Finding out this information and making contact with employers from your home are reasons why job searchers are rushing to the Internet. All kinds of jobs are being filled from postings in every imaginable field.

As employers climb onto the Internet bandwagon, they welcome (and may even expect) that candidates will be looking for them on the World Wide Web. In fact, an Internet site, once it's up and running, costs only a few hundred dollars to maintain. Traditional newspaper employment advertising may cost thousands for a single ad, and a headhunter's search may cost several thousand dollars.

Another advantage for organizations is the quality of the applicants they get from those who are willing to navigate the information superhighway. An e-mail address, a personal home page or a resume posted on-line are viewed as indicators that an applicant is willing to move into the future, use resources creatively and stay competitive in the marketplace.

A third area of major importance (and cost-saving potential for employers) is that an on-line candidate requires less "space." More and more human resource departments are going digital: scanning paper resumes into a database that can be searched for key words or skills when openings occur. The paperwork of hiring is an expensive, time-consuming, space-demanding challenge for both large and small organizations.

When you use the Internet to job search, your resume doesn't sit on someone's desk in a stack with hundreds of others. Your challenge will be how to be selected out of a database, not how to make your resume look better or how to find a gimmick that attracts attention. Section 3 will help you develop a resume that works in this new way. You'll also need to change your thinking about interviews, perhaps using an electronic portfolio to present your skills and experience.

When you complete the reading and exercises and begin to build a career plan, you may find some areas of discomfort—things you never thought about—or you may find yourself thinking that it's all too complicated. An effective career plan is not achieved overnight. That's why this book offers you ideas and support in many areas of the career transition process: defining your market based on your dreams, researching the possibilities, presenting your skills and accomplishments as well as the tools to access electronic communication resources. Use it in combination with resources listed in the bibliography to explore specific topics.

Most important, this book will help you get the information you need to file your resume with thousands of employers without spending a dime on a phone call. It's easy to build your own career-net, so get going!

Carrie Straub

e-mail: *carries@us.world.net*

snailmail: *Resources for Success*
              7119 N. Washburne
              Portland, OR 97217
              Phone: 503-286-1252

SECTION

1

Deciding On Your Next Job or Career

After you read and complete the exercises in this section you should be able to:

- *Identify your skills, experience, and accomplishments*
- *Clarify your values and dreams and how they relate to work*
- *Identify how your transferable skills and resulting accomplishments are linked to various industries of interest*
- *Overcome common barriers to an effective job search*

For most of us, work is a key element in defining who we are and how we feel about ourselves. The most difficult job search may be for people who have been forced to leave a job they liked (or even a job they didn't like but felt secure with) and redefine themselves as individuals instead of as an analyst or manager or what have you.

Work helps us to realize our dreams and ambitions. Some people trade time for money so that they can pursue their hobbies or raise their families in surroundings compatible with their values. Work allows us to contribute to our community and, in some cases, may indicate the value the community places on that contribution. Some of us do unpaid work to gain skills, realize some talent or satisfy other needs.

In his book *Regain Your Focus After Losing Your Job,* author Richard Koonce says, "Losing a job is one of the most stressful things that can happen to a person. In fact, psychologists rank it as No. 3 on the stress list, after "the death of a loved one and divorce." He offers advice for job seekers, which is as valid for those who are searching from inclination as from necessity. Koonce urges planning, gathering information and a resume that markets your skills as critical ingredients to any job search.

Today's organizations build marketing plans to help them answer the following questions:

1. What can they expect from a product?
2. Who will buy the product?
3. What will consumers pay for it?
4. Who is the competition?
5. Where could the product be sold?
6. What is the cost of production?

Whether you are seeking your first job, job searching because your employer is "right-sizing" or some other event, or making a determined effort to develop a career that is more satisfying, you will need to create a marketing plan of your own. That plan begins with an assessment of the product you want to offer in the job market, and that assessment needs to include the following:

■ Your skills and experience
■ Your education and affiliations
■ Your accomplishments
■ Your values, dreams and cultural emphasis

- Your willingness to give up some things that may have been present in recent employment

You can develop strategies to market yourself by completing the exercises in this book, thinking about and discussing the answers and issues generated by the exercises and becoming familiar with the electronic tools that will help you complete your job search. By linking the ideas generated by this book with the resources you already have, you will discover new horizons, and you'll have developed new skills that can be a foundation for the rest of your career.

PLANNING YOUR JOB SEARCH

Often overlooked, planning is the key to any job or career change. Most people spend more time planning a vacation than they do their careers. This is especially true when it comes to defining their qualifications. Richard Koonce, author of *Career Power!*, suggests several ingredients for successful career moves. Two of the most crucial, and yet neglected, are:

- Commit yourself to continuous learning throughout your entire working life.
- Learn how to "suitcase" your skills and leverage your experience. Be ready to pack up and take your qualifications with you on a moment's notice.

 Exercise: Identifying Your Skills and Experience

Your marketing plan should begin with an assessment of your product. Use the following chart to list the skills and abilities you have now and those you need to build. Note those that are specific to an individual employer or to an industry different from the one in which you now work.

Skills I Have Now	Abilities I Bring to the Job Market	Skills I Need to Build

You also need to define any areas in which you have skills that you don't want to market. For example, perhaps you are an excellent bookkeeper but want to work with people and use your sales skills. Minimize experience you don't want to use.

List below the experience or skills you don't want to market:

_____

_____

_____

The Bottom Line

Write a brief statement that describes your perfect job: What strengths would you use? What challenges might be present? What would you learn?

_____

_____

_____

Wouldn't it be wonderful if all we had to do was assess what we want and, magically, that job would be available? And wouldn't it be even more wonderful if once we got the job, we found it as satisfying as we had thought it would be? Chances are that most of us have to endure some trials and errors, finding out what we want to do, what we don't want to do, and finding a comfortable combination within a setting that satisfies us most of the time while still providing for growth and challenge.

Providing Evidence of Your Traits and Skills

Marci Mahoney's book *Strategic Resumes* offers an effective formula for writing statements that give evidence of your accomplishments instead of listing tasks or responsibilities. The following table shows some examples:

Trait/Skill	Evidence of Your Accomplishments
Interpret and clarify building codes for the public	Researched building codes and developed recommendations for city adoption; identified and reviewed state and federal laws that affected codes Developed and published "plain language" statements that ensured understanding by clients and reduced application turnaround time.
Dependable	When assigned a project that had been given top priority but had not been accomplished, I collaborated with other supervisors to complete the project while our manager was on leave.

Now it's your turn to define your traits and skills and provide evidence that you have them (that is, show that you've made accomplishments in these areas). Remember to focus only on those traits and skills that you want to sell. If your resume includes things you don't want to do anymore, you'll get another job just like the one you want to leave! And in this exercise, the phrase "responsible for" is off limits!

Trait/Skill	Evidence of Your Accomplishments

Your Education and Affiliations Are Assets

Formal education is a real asset to any career change. However, employers tend to be more interested in what you have produced. There's also a "recency" factor. A 20-year-old Bachelor's degree may not be as valuable as the ability to produce $2 million per year in commissionable sales or to negotiate labor relations contracts successfully.

Define your formal education in terms of training or school. List your professional affiliations that increase your knowledge of your job or industry.

Education and Training	Professional Activities/Affiliations

Identifying Your Accomplishments

Getting ready to post your resume on-line or send it via e-mail takes some work. Because you will want to show you are a *producer,* write about the *results* of your work, not the tasks for which you were responsible. Earlier in this chapter, you defined your job skills and noted some evidence that you have those skills. You will find many uses for those definitions as you take your job search on-line, for example, in your cover letters to prospective employers, or as part of your personal Web page.

The next step is to define the difference those skills made to the work you were doing. For example,

- *"Defined needs for new work-flow process and implemented changes that saved $50,000 in 12 months."*

- *"Initiated fundraising event that raised over $5,000 for local high school prom night. This included arranging to have home owners offer garden tours, coordinating volunteer guides and gaining publicity from newspapers and TV stations."*

- *"Created job search progress team that resulted in 12 members being employed within a 60-day period."*

Here are shells for some sample statements. Fill in the blanks of those that apply to your own situation.

- Identified [_____] and [_____]. Resulted
  PROBLEM   DESCRIBE SOLUTION
  in [_____].
  QUANTIFIABLE RESULT

- Suggested new [_____], which [_____
  PROCESS, PROCEDURE, IDEA   SAVED TIME,
  _____] for [_____
  MADE IT EASIER, COST LESS, INCREASED ACCURACY   GROUP, TEAM,
  _____].
  CUSTOMER

- Eliminated [_____] backlog of [_____
  QUANTITY, LENGTH OF TIME ORDERS,
  _____] while keeping incoming work current.
  RECORDS, FILES

- Consolidated [_____], generating a savings of
  DEPARTMENTS, TASKS
  [_____].
  TIME, DOLLARS, AND SO ON

- Reduced [_____] by [_____] in
  ERRORS, COSTS, TIME SPENT ON TASK QUANTITY
  [_____].
  LENGTH OF TIME

The key to writing accomplishment statements is to

- Keep statements brief and to the point
- Use active verbs and eliminate the phrases "reported to" or "responsible for"
- Show improvement that is measured (you can decide what the measurement is) by results that are significant to the job you are seeking
- Highlight the things you like to do or want to do in your next job

Exercise: Your Accomplishment Statements Worksheet

List your eight greatest work-related accomplishments, four from each of your last two jobs. These can be from paid or unpaid work, and they can be people-, idea- or technology-oriented. Use the format and tips described earlier.

Most recent job: —————————————————————————

Title: ———————————————————————————————

Accomplishments:

1. ——————————————————————————————————

   ——————————————————————————————————

2. ——————————————————————————————————

   ——————————————————————————————————

3. ——————————————————————————————————

   ——————————————————————————————————

4. ——————————————————————————————————

   ——————————————————————————————————

Previous job: ————————————————————————————

Title: ———————————————————————————————

Accomplishments:

5. ——————————————————————————————————

   ——————————————————————————————————

6. ——————————————————————————————————

   ——————————————————————————————————

7. ——————————————————————————————————

   ——————————————————————————————————

8. ——————————————————————————————————

   ——————————————————————————————————

NOTE: Go to *http://www.jobtrak.com/jobmanual/assess.html* to get ideas about competencies.

Exercise: Clarifying Your Values and Dreams

Your values and dreams are two important issues to consider as you decide on your next job or career. In this exercise, list five to seven of the important values and dreams that affect your decisions about your work. (You may wish to discuss this exercise with someone who knows you well. You can do that electronically via e-mail so that you aren't limited to the people in your immediate area.)

List these values and dreams in the order of priority as they affect your decisions. For instance, if an important value for you is to be where you can enjoy many cultures, it would probably affect your willingness to move to a small community with a single predominant culture. Try *http://www.bgsu.edu/offices/careers/process/exercise.html* for help in this area.

Priority	Important Values and Dreams	How They Affect My Job Search Decisions
1.		
2.		
3.		
4.		
5.		
6.		
7.		

There are no wrong answers in this exercise. There are only answers that are wrong for you.

Using the results of this exercise:

- Compare the answers from this exercise to the skills, accomplishments and abilities you decide to offer to an employer.

- Use your answers from this exercise to develop questions to present to any on-line discussion groups in which you participate.

- Use the answers from this exercise when you develop your personal commercial and when you create your cover letter or introductory statements in your on-line resume (covered in Section 3).

- Consider your answers when you review job descriptions posted on-line or read what companies have to say about their culture. For example, if a description says, "Fast-paced high-tech start-up, state of the art, ever-challenging environment," and your values statement says, "time to devote to my family, able to complete one project before starting another," that job probably is not the right one for you.

 Exercise: The Ideal Workplace

It's time now to review some of the elements in your ideal workplace that will satisfy most of your needs and to figure out what you can live without in other, less wonderful settings. It's called *quality of life,* and although you may apply that concept to life outside of work, how often do you apply it while searching for a job? What would make your work life most satisfying?

List the things that you really want to have present in your next workplace, and then think about some indicators that will prove those elements are present. List four issues you feel strongly about.

Important Workplace Environment Issue	Proof This Element Is Present
Example: employee empowerment	Example: flexible work hours; decisions made at lowest level; Internet access available to all*

*In Company O, an electronics wholesale firm, the information systems manager was showing me his state-of-the-art computer training classroom, which included Internet access. I asked, "How many of your employees use the Internet?" He replied, "Only seven or eight. We just can't take a chance on having them 'playing' around." What would this suggest about employee empowerment in this company? (These folks sell phone systems, computers and Internet connection equipment, and want to be considered the distributor of the future.)

Using the results of this exercise:

- Use these indicators to evaluate what is said on-line about any companies you are considering as an employer.

- Develop statements about yourself based on these elements. Read between the lines of a company's Web page to see if your definition of empowerment matches theirs.

Exercise: Reflecting on Your Career

Use the following chart to reflect on your career, considering two years at a time. Make a brief list under each column heading for the most recent two-year segment of your career. Draw a line across the page under the longest list, and then make a list in each column for the previous two-year segment. Examine up to the past ten years of your career (ie, look at up to five two-year segments).

Using the results of this exercise:

■ Obtain the e-mail addresses of your career mentors, and find out if they are willing to become part of your on-line support team or if they can provide links to other mentors (see Internetworking in Section 2).

 ## *Exercise: Career-Related Experience Profile*

This exercise will help you answer the question, "Why Should We Hire You As [Job Title] At Our Company?" Complete this exercise by defining a career or job title that interests you or where you know an opening exists, and then profile your experience as it applies to that job. If possible, do this exercise on your computer so that you start to build a database about your experience. Do it for as many jobs as you can.

Job _____

_____

_____

Reflecting on Your Career

Dates (in 2-year segments starting about 10 years ago)	What did you learn?	What was your job/career/ avocation?	What did you do for leisure?	Who were your mentors, guides or advisors?	How did they help?	What could they still help you with?

My experience (write a career summary stressing your years of experience and the range of duties and responsibilities you have had that prepare you for the job you have defined above):

_____

_____

_____

_____

My relevant technical skills and/or knowledge:

_____

_____

My accomplishments and proven track record:

_____

_____

My education or managerial skills:

_____

_____

My general talents and abilities:

_____

_____

My personal attributes and strengths:

_____

_____

THE CHANGING FACE OF THE JOB MARKET

If you are ready to take responsibility for presenting yourself to the 1990s workplace, the next issues may well be that of company size and maturity. Examine your attitude about working for a start-up, a small firm or an entrepreneur. For the past several years, small businesses have created most of the new jobs in our economy. About 37 percent of those small businesses are owned by women, accounting for about 8 million companies and a contribution of $2.3 trillion to the economy.

Where do I get these numbers? The Labor Statistics site at *http://stats.bls.gov/*. This Web site is a treasure trove of data about growing industries, projections about salaries and market statistics. So, defining the job market does not mean reading the Sunday classifieds. Times have changed.

Finding the right buyer for your skills and experience will happen faster if you do the research and target employers that measure up to your criteria. The Internet provides almost unlimited resources for this type of activity.

Start by reviewing the information you have collected in the exercises so far. Choose the type of employer and location you think will fit. Keep this information in mind as you search directories, trade associations, on-line newspapers and magazines and other on-line resources to target companies that fit your criteria.

Call, write or e-mail the firms you target. Their public relations departments will send annual reports, product brochures and names of people who head up the departments. If the company is privately owned, it may not publish an annual report, so ask for a press kit or other information. If you are interested in the international scene, you will be able to obtain government reports from many countries. (Some are available in English; some are not.)

Now you will be more able to present your experience in terms of results and accomplishments instead of responsibilities and tasks, in relation to an organization's specific goals and priorities.

 ## Exercise: Overcoming the Speed Bumps

Review the list below, and determine which of these issues might affect your job search—that is, which are "speed bumps" that will slow you down in finding the job you want or moving into a new field. Work through these perceived barriers with a friend, or post them as questions on-line to get feedback and ideas from others. Gather at least three ideas for responding to each item on your list.

Barrier or "Speed Bump"	Ideas for Overcoming This Barrier
Young/inexperienced/job title doesn't reflect level of experience	
Re-entry to workforce or most experience in volunteer work	
Older	
Frequent job changes	
Same job for more than five years	
Gap in work history	
Fired from job	
Negative reference from previous supervisor	
Little formal education	
Present salary above range/overqualified	
Any other barriers you perceive:	

Putting a Positive Spin on the Barriers

Which interview question are you most concerned about answering?

_____

_____

_____

_____

Use the ideas you gathered in the previous exercise to develop an answer to this question. Write down your answer so that you can incorporate it in your cover letter or resume.

_____

_____

_____

_____

Remember, focus on what you *do* have and how you can benefit an employer instead of what you don't have.

Did you run out of ideas? Why work on this alone? Now is the time to

- Post a question on a listserv for some career or industry that interests you
- Read an article from an on-line resource to get new ideas and expand your answers
- Use a bulletin board to make connections with others in the city, company or job area you are exploring

JUMP-STARTING A STALLED JOB SEARCH

■ Turn rejections into learning experiences by using your job search network (that is, your in-person and on-line connections for career guidance—see Internetworking in Section 2) to get feedback about your resume, your interview or your industry knowledge.

■ Use the Internet to get an informational interview. It may not be practical to meet with a given individual at a company you're targeting (eg, a regional sales manager, who is in town only rarely), so try contacting the individual by e-mail, and if you get a favorable response, send a list of questions you'd like answered.

Remember that Jay Leno had a fifth-grade teacher who said, "If Jay spent as much time studying as he does trying to be a comedian, he'd be a big star!" and that Mickey Mantle struck out 710 times. The resources on the Internet will help you broaden the scope of your search, add interest and give you new, salable skills. Don't be afraid to use them.

SECTION

2

Developing Your Personal Marketing Plan

After you read and complete the exercises in this section you should be able to:

- *Assess some of the job search strategies that you will use for your search*
- *Develop a list of at least five URLs that you will visit during your Internet job search*
- *Develop an objectives list, assign realistic dates for completion, brainstorm a to-do task list for each objective and assign priorities*
- *Ask for help from a variety of networking sources, both in person and on-line*

In hiring, today's employers have three basic questions:

1. Can you do the job?
2. Will you do the job?
3. Will you produce more than you cost?

These three questions can be summarized in one: "Why should we hire you as [JOB TITLE] at our company?" This suggests that you had better know what employers are looking for, what you are bringing to the table and how to present your capabilities more effectively than any other candidate. Today's electronic tools give the job seeker a running start, and new tools are emerging every day. Before you begin the process of marketing yourself on-line you should do five key things:

1. Plan to do research on-line.
2. Get organized.
3. Set goals, objectives and time targets.
4. Ask for help, input and "air time" with others.
5. Be realistic about the amount of time you have to devote to changing careers or changing jobs.

The rest of this section explores these items in more detail.

 ## KEY #1. PLAN TO DO RESEARCH ON-LINE

Researching on-line has two benefits. First, by using the Internet, you gain hands-on familiarity with a tool that is taking the business world by storm. Challenge yourself to try out the search engines, push the limits in searching for information on topics and visit the sites recommended in this book.

As with any marketing project, you have the highest chance of success when you have targeted

- A specific audience
- With needs you can fill
- Who will give you the opportunity to apply the skills/ experience/talents you most enjoy using to a job you find challenging and that fits your values

So much information is available from the resources on the Internet that you could easily become overwhelmed and lose your motivation. Focus your job search on the Internet with the following steps:

■ Pay a "virtual visit" to companies that interest you and bookmark their sites so that you can return there easily.

■ Identify industry-related Web sites using the same search techniques.

■ Search for listservs that represent people in the profession or industry you want to explore or in which you wish to network.

List three industries or professions 1) you feel would offer a positive image for you and 2) are growing or will grow in the future:

_____

_____

_____

List five to seven specific skills or experiences that you could transfer into those industries or professions:

_____

_____

_____

_____

_____

_____

_____

Staying Focused

The Internet can be fascinating. Surfing—or simply following links from site to site—can consume a lot of time. You will need to sort out the enormous amount of information you can access. You will find distractions of all kinds and could spend an entire day (or night) on-line, with nothing to show for it. These distractions can get out of control, diverting you from searching for a job. The following tips will help you stay focused:

- Set up a to-do list for your sessions. This will help you stay on track, getting the information you need and producing results for your search.

- Decide in advance what information you are looking for. Resist the temptation to follow links from the original site. Instead, bookmark the original site, give yourself a specific amount of time to visit the site or follow links, and then come back to your research.

- Allot some casual surfing time. You know what other obligations you have. Decide how long you can spend playing. Even during this time, it's wise to keep your goals in front of you so that what you do still applies to your search.

- Use the "push" technology described in this book to get the information delivered to you (see Resources for Market Research in Section 4).

- Unsubscribe from lists that don't produce for you. Downloading and reading 50 nonrelevant e-mail messages is not the best use of your time. If you need to stay subscribed to stay up-to-date, make a file and spend a specific amount of time doing the reading.

- Set up a file system of mailboxes for your e-mail messages. Download your e-mail, answer and file it. Group all the e-mails on a specific topic or from a certain person, and then transfer them to your file mailboxes all at once, deleting those of no interest.

- Set up your browser to bring up the home page of the newspaper whose classifieds you find most useful or of your professional association. Simple to do, this will keep your target in front of you.

- Stay out of chat rooms and avoid doing other nonessential on-line activities, or use those activities as rewards for getting specific tasks done and out of the way.

- Be aware of your "body clock"—if your energy is low in the evening, get up an hour earlier and use your best creative time to do the tasks.

- Have a plan. Job searching is work: know what you want to accomplish, do that and get off line.

 ### *Action Item*

Visit the site at *http://www.paradesa.com* and check out the Digging for Data section of Learn the Net.

 ## KEY #2. GET ORGANIZED

Sticky notes on the light switch and phone numbers and URLs jotted down on the back of your birthday card won't help you feel productive. At the very least, you will need to learn to set up file folders (for storing mail) within your e-mail program, bookmark sites you want to visit frequently, and use a three-ring binder with tabs to organize research about companies and contacts.

Since your odyssey may take you to distant companies and evolve over the next months or years, start as you want to continue. Build habits that will make it easy for you to spend time on essential career management functions instead of devoting half a day to searching for contact information that you put on the back of a take-out menu.

Creating Your Own Cyberaddress Book

Use material in this section to

- Create and organize your electronic job search addresses
- Record addresses that you get when you aren't near your computer
- Track contact dates and keep your list current
- Prepare data for entry into your computer-based system
- Minimize lost information and searching for the best contact you've made

Create a Contact Log

- Make two photocopies of the next page and use the two copies to make a master contact sheet (containing two columns of contacts). Photocopy the master onto three-hole-punched paper. Put these pages behind alphabetized tabs.
- Consider color-coding the pages by whatever logic seems appropriate to you—for example, using blue paper for places where you can post your resume, green for addresses of local associations, and so on.
- Use a standard three-ring binder or your personal organizer binder, whichever will make it easier for you to use the information.

Name:

Title:

Address:

Phone: FAX:

e-mail:

URL:

Contact Dates/Referral Source:

Name:

Title:

Address:

Phone: FAX:

e-mail:

URL:

Contact Dates/Referral Source:

Name:

Title:

Address:

Phone: FAX:

e-mail:

URL:

Contact Dates/Referral Source:

Name:

Title:

Address:

Phone: FAX:

e-mail:

URL:

Contact Dates/Referral Source:

Better yet, take another step into the future! Why use a low-tech way to keep track of high-tech resources? You will want to spend more time collecting resources than organizing them on paper, and figuring out which site is which often requires more searching than it's worth. As sites move and new URLs replace old ones, an electronic address book format may be a simpler way to keep track of these resources.

Some of the best solutions may already be on your computer. New technology in datebooks, laptop calendar planners, or palmtop machines allows you to download information onto your computer. Use these features to become a premier net-worker. Staying in touch with prospective employers doesn't happen by accident.

Create a URL Log

Bookmarking the Web sites you visit as you explore the Internet is the most efficient way to work. That way you will be able to go back again and again very quickly. However, your collection of URLs will probably grow from other sources as well (for example, networking contacts, newspaper or magazine articles or ads, or even informal discussions on noncareer-related subjects). So much information is available that it's critical to stay organized. Creating a URL log is also a good idea, so that you can keep track of the resources available at various URLs, even when you're away from your computer. Following is a sample and some suggested uses for such a log:

URL	For

■ Copy this page onto heavy card stock and include it in the various sections of your job search binder to organize specific information for each industry.

■ Laminate a copy of this page and use it with an erasable marker to note possibilities as you read newspaper or magazine articles.

■ Take a copy to a networking meeting or professional association and ask each person you meet to add a URL.

Action Item

Open the following locations and bookmark/hotlist them:

> *http://www.monster.com*
>
> *http://www.careermosaic.com*
>
> *http://www.jobhunt.org*

 ## KEY #3. SET GOALS, OBJECTIVES AND TIME TARGETS

By defining a target date for completing specific goals, no matter how arbitrary, you transform wannabes into realities. You start a process that gets you moving toward your goal. Use a project management approach to your search. An Activity Network Diagram, an example of which follows, is a common tool for scheduling sequential and simultaneous tasks.

Creating an On-line Job Search Activity Network Diagram

Developing an Activity Network Diagram helps you set targets for activities. When you have a general goal such as "get a new job," it's easy to procrastinate. By defining the specific actions that you must take, you can begin to accomplish the small steps that will get you to your target. You can decide which steps you need to complete. For example,

1. Define your main objective (eg, "Change jobs").

2. Brainstorm a list of all tasks that must be done to meet that objective. Record your main objective and the required tasks on Post-it notes or on index cards.

3. Place your objective to the extreme left on a sheet of paper that is large enough to accommodate all the tasks.

4. Review the tasks to identify which must be done first, which may be done simultaneously and which require the completion of an earlier task. Number the tasks accordingly. Use consecutive numbers to indicate tasks that must be done in order. If tasks may be done simultaneously, assign the tasks a-b-c designations to indicate that they are all part of the same time sequence.

5. Place tasks that may be done simultaneously in the same horizontal position (that is, next to each other) on the diagram. Tasks that must be done sequentially should be placed in the same horizontal position on the diagram (with the first task on top and subsequent tasks below).

6. Decide on a realistic time frame for completing each task and indicate the task deadlines on the diagram.

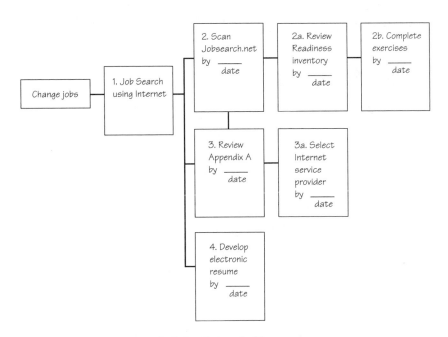

Activity Network Diagram

7. Identify any forgotten tasks, assess what challenges you may face.

8. Get going. The resources on the Internet are multiplying like crazy.

It's important to state a goal, identify the steps you will take to reach that goal and assign timelines. Otherwise, it's easy to get frustrated or discouraged. So much information is available, you can become sidetracked. As you prepare your action plan, be as specific as possible about the steps. It's okay to set a new date for a step as long as you are working on it. If you set a date and miss it because of procrastination, talk to someone in your job search network about strategies for staying on track with your transition.

Career transition goal(s):

Date	By this date, I will accomplish the following action steps:

 *Action Item*

Develop an objectives list, assign realistic dates for completion, brainstorm a to-do task list for each objective and assign priorities.

 ## KEY #4. ASK FOR HELP, INPUT AND "AIR TIME" WITH OTHERS

On-line career centers are not just for resume/job posting. Visit their career coaching and information sections, post to mail lists and ask questions. You have the ability to network globally. Take advantage of it. Staying connected keeps you going if the job search gets tough.

The U.S. Department of Labor conducted a survey to determine how American workers found jobs. The study included 10.4 million people and included all categories of wage and salary workers from blue collar to managerial and professional. The survey showed that about 64 percent found their jobs through networking, and about 15 percent found jobs via advertised openings.

If you send a resume to a random list of employers, odds are 2 in 100 that you'll get an interview. If you network, the odds are 10 in 100—five times better. Other statistics show that on average it takes contact with 28 hiring managers to be hired. It will take five times longer to get in front of those hiring managers if you aren't networking.

Internetworking should support—not supplant—your person-to-person networking activities. A key advantage of using the Internet for networking is that it allows you to be active even when you have only a few minutes to spare or if you can't get to a specific meeting because of travel or timing.

Networking Market Quiz

Read the following statements and check off whether you believe they are true or false. Answers follow.

True **False**

☐ ☐ 1. On average, an employer takes less than a minute to read a resume for the first time.

☐ ☐ 2. The only way to get in to see a hiring manager is through a job interview.

☐ ☐ 3. Employers are turned off when contacted by job seekers.

☐ ☐ 4. Seventy-five to 80 percent of all jobs filled are found through the "hidden" (unpublished) job market.

☐ ☐ 5. Seventy-five percent of all jobs could be learned by most people in three weeks or less.

☐ ☐ 6. More than 70 percent of all jobs obtained are found through want ads.

☐ ☐ 7. It is not good practice to ask friends and relatives for employer contacts.

☐ ☐ 8. There is a real, available job behind every position that is listed in the postings or classified ads.

☐ ☐ 9. Of the 75 to 80 percent of jobs found in the hidden job market, about one-third of them are created specifically for the job seeker who has successfully made a contact within the hidden market.

Answers to Networking Market Quiz
1. T (So make it a good one!) **2.** F **3.** F **4.** T **5.** T (Too many employers look for a perfect match, but showing your capacity to learn is a big plus.) **6.** F **7.** F (Tell everyone you can!) **8.** F (Companies are sometimes just testing the market.) **9.** T

Tips for Successful Internetworking

- Visit sites that list associations, discussion or interest groups or user groups that might know about jobs in your field or industry.

- Subscribe to listservs and read them for a few weeks. Post to them when you have something of interest to say or a question you would like discussed.

- Collect e-mail addresses of people you connect with at "live" functions.

- Surf the Web and e-mail comments or questions to the Web master at sites that catch your interest.

- Visit Web sites of companies in your industry. Read about how they prefer to receive resumes, what jobs they have open and how they identify themselves in the market.

- Develop a few personal commercials that have been spell-checked, edited and can be cut-and-pasted into your messages as needed (see Section 3). These should be snippets of information about you that are clear, concise and easy to include when developing written replies.

- Neatness counts! On-line postings show your writting skills. Spelling errors, typos and grammatical slips are not allowed. If your resume says you have excellent written communication skills, it should show in your on-line posting.

- Become a "switchboard," passing along information about jobs or industry issues to others.
- Give information . . . do not expect that you will only be the recipient. Contribute to on-line forums.
- Pay attention *all the time.* A strong network can be important for doing your job, or advancing your career.
- Create a personal business card that you can give out.
- Create a matching on-line business card "signature" for your e-mail (see Section 3).

 ### *Exercise: Brainstorm the Possibilities*

Jot down names or immediate possibilities for a start at internetworking:

Internet Tool	Activity	Names, Possibilities
e-mail	■ Stay in contact with former associates, friends and family at very low cost ■ Write to trade journals and professional associations for lists of employers ■ Send resume to newspaper ads that list e-mail addresses ■ Request information about products and projects from Web sites	
listserv	■ Subscribe to and read mail lists of interest (from industry or functional perspective) for one week ■ Contribute ideas or answer questions ■ Ask for information about places to post resumes or make contacts	
Usenet newsgroups	■ Search newsgroups for discussion groups of interest ■ Post articles or comments ■ Ask for information	

Action Item

Visit your local library and review its Internet and other on-line resources for job searching.

 KEY #5. BE REALISTIC ABOUT THE TIME YOU CAN DEVOTE

A complete career change may be a two-to-five-year project, especially if you will need to gain experience or return to school to complete a degree. A job search could take anywhere from a few weeks to many months. Nothing on the Internet will replace the work of job searching. It just gives you a wider reach and new, more efficient tools. It's been said that "Luck is when preparation and opportunity meet." You may spend eight hours a day while in the job search mode, creating your electronic resume, developing contacts and using the tools, or you may spend a few hours a week, staying tapped in to opportunities until the right one comes along.

 Action Item

Start a log of the hours you spend working on some part of your job search goals. If you usually invest an extra two hours per day in your current job, begin to invest that time in exploring alternative job opportunities and career preparation.

SECTION

3

Marketing Yourself On-Line

After you read and complete the exercises in this section you should be able to:

- *Define some of the key words you will want to include in your resume*

- *Develop an ASCII text resume that will represent you well on-line*

- *Create an electronic cover letter to accompany your resume*

- *Decide how you will configure your e-mail address*

- *Evaluate some of the risks in sending a document as an "attachment"*

- *Identify some of the basic principles of Netiquette*

Research shows that for every 1,470 resumes sent out, only *one* results in the candidate's landing a job! That means that if your resume isn't a winner, it's a killer! A resume isn't an obituary; it's a sales tool with a job to do. That job is to get an employer to pick up the phone and schedule you for an interview, to get you pulled out of a database and into the pool of candidates to be considered, and to represent you in a positive way to the employment world.

Today's resume needs to answer the "Why should I hire you?" question quickly and easily. It needs to contain key words that will get you selected from an electronic database, show accomplishments that prove you will produce more than you cost and make it easy for the hiring manager to figure out what you really did in your previous jobs.

CREATING AN ON-LINE RESUME

Although your on-line resume may contain the same information as your paper one, it will have some key differences. Addressing those differences means a significant shift in the way you think about the document you're creating. When you build an electronic resume, you aren't working on a piece of paper. It won't sit in a stack on someone's desk or be stored in a file. This is an interactive resource for "discovery." Do the research required to assure you will be selected out of a company's database. Stay current with industry buzzwords, select key words carefully and show accomplishments and initiative.

Developing a Key-Word Section

Your resume will be stored in a database from which information (resumes of likely candidates) will be extracted via a "query" based on key words. The best way to communicate your qualifications is to use key words and concepts that have an impact on the audience and trigger immediate interest in your product—*you*. The use of these words will ensure that your resume is pulled out of the database that is being searched for specific skills or experience. The more key words your resume contains, the greater the likelihood that your resume will be forwarded to a manager for consideration.

The following list will help you get started; however, it is not all-inclusive. After you have reviewed the following key words and concepts (and added others in the final column), circle the ones that apply to you. Use the blanks to add any characteristics that are unique to you, your job or industry.

Technical and/or Managerial Skills Key Words

management/ supervision	cost containment/ cost reduction	real estate financing
project management	return on investment evaluation	lead entry into markets
budget development	quality orientation	market definition
recruiting	continuous improvement	proven excellent judgment
training	international operations	strong operations/ administration experience
mediation	acquisitions/ mergers	computer literate (Internet literate)
team building		
territory development	grant proposal development	organizational ability
strategic planning	concept-to-implementation project management	negotiating skills
problem definition analysis		research skills
systems development	operations planning	verbal communication
systems administration	change management	public speaking/ presentations

speak/read/write
fluent [language]

_____

detail oriented

_____

makes on the spot
decisions

_____

brings order out
of chaos

_____

superior technical
competence

_____

strong people
skills

_____

strong leader and
team-builder

_____

problem solving

_____

streamlined
operations

_____

established
priorities

_____

rejuvenated failing
efforts

_____

spearheaded new
projects

_____

 *Action Item*

Practice using directories and search engines such as Yahoo or Infoseek. Notice anything? Sometimes a term that seems appropriate to you may not be the one an employer uses (for example, in some places, the person who does the "generalist" work is called a "specialist," and sometimes a "coordinator" is really a project manager).

Read job descriptions carefully, and develop a key word list targeted for the company to which you are sending your resume. When posting a resume to a generalized site, use your glossary or thesaurus to assure that you have included appropriate synonyms.

ASCII Text Resume Format

An ASCII text resume is a necessity for an on-line job search. It is relatively easy to create if you have done your content homework well. Computers made it easy for candidates to create printed resumes that sometimes paid more attention to format than content, but when it comes to on-line resumes, the simpler the better. To follow are two sample resumes. The first is an ASCII text resume, and the second has the bells and whistles of a more traditional, graphically enhanced resume: same content, different formats.

Human resources departments have long endorsed one-page resumes, not because that format represents the applicant particularly well, but because it reduces the department's need to read, store and process or, perhaps, fax, an additional page or two of information on each candidate.

Your Name
Your Address
Your e-mail/URL

KEY WORDS

Put the key words up front because the text is searched from beginning to end, and the sooner the "hit" takes place, the more quickly your resume will be identified as one that should be included.

EXPERIENCE

Current or most recent employer   Dates of employment

Title of your most recent position

A brief description of the situation in your current or most recent employment, for example, size of department, goal of unit, key products or some indication of magnitude.

ASCII Text Resume

Your Name
Your Address
Your e-mail/URL

KEY WORDS

Put the key words up front because the text is searched from beginning to end, and the sooner the "hit" takes place, the more quickly your resume will be identified as one that should be included.

EXPERIENCE

Current or most recent employer   *Dates of employment*

Title of your most recent position

A brief description of the situation in your current or most recent employment, for example, size of department, goal of unit, key products or some indication of magnitude.

Traditional Resume

Most recruiting departments are turning to technology to save the day. Internet technology is being used to transmit applications and resumes. Document imaging, which eliminates the human assessment of qualifications and matches candidates to jobs, is crucial to most companies. An ASCII text resume can be "cut and pasted" into an e-mail document, eliminating the need to send it as an attachment.

Scannable Resume Format

The most common scanning device used for storing resumes into an electronic applicant tracking system is the Optical Character Reader (OCR). These machines are mixed blessings.

They get resumes stored where they can be accessed quickly, clear up the backlog experienced by the recruiting department, and level the playing field for everyone by minimizing the human factor in resume review. They automatically add you to the database, even date-stamping your information with the dates your resume was received and entered. They allow your resume to be stored for longer periods of time and help you be considered for jobs you didn't know existed.

On the other hand, these readers can err, misreading the Y's on your resume and turning them into V's or misinterpreting the typeface you selected, relegating your entire resume to a collection of I's and O's. Machine readers might run the section headings into body text; they can stall at underlining, boldface type or poor contrast, turning your resume into an indecipherable file.

Your Name
Your Address
Your e-mail/URL

KEY WORDS

Put the key words up front because the text is searched from beginning to end, and the sooner the "hit" takes place, the more quickly your resume will be identified as one that should be included.

EXPERIENCE

Current or most recent employer   Dates of employment

Title of your most recent position

A brief description of the situation in your current or most recent employment, for example, size of department, goal of unit, key products or some indication of magnitude.

■ List 3–4 accomplishments, in bulleted format. Bullets must be filled in and dark because scanners tend to read hollow bullets or boxes as the letter "O."

Previous/Next most recent employer   Dates of employment

Title

Repeat the format above. This time, use only one or two accomplishments, unless you were in this position for several years, and the most recent position was of shorter duration.

EDUCATION

List your degrees, training or skills updates in this section. If your education is newly completed and it is your primary qualification for the job, move this section to follow Key Words.

PROFESSIONAL AFFILIATIONS/ACHIEVEMENTS/AWARDS

Keep this section confined to the past three to five years (unless it was a Rhodes scholarship, presidential citation, Olympic medal or the like) and, for the most part, to job-related activities, organizations or awards. Your activities in the local chapter of the Basketweavers Guild need not be included, unless you are applying for a marketing manager position at a basket manufacturing company. The bonus you received for three years in a row as a result of your creative efforts for the United Way Loaned Executive program belongs here.

Scannable Resume

If you want to be sure your resume gets you into the database:

- Produce a version of your resume that has no lines or boldface and that uses only upper- and lowercase characters. Avoid using shadowed or reversed typefaces. Yes, it looks plain vanilla. The thing is, the OCR *likes* plain vanilla.

- Use a standard type font such as Geneva, Arial or Helvetica in the sans serif family. If you prefer a serif style type font, use Palatino, Times or New Century Schoolbook. You can mix fonts for effect, but use no more than two fonts, or the resume will take on a patchwork look. Don't condense spacing between letters.

- Use a font size between 10 and 14 points.

- Print your resume on light colored paper (white is best, but pale gray or ivory may work). Use a laser printer for maximum contrast. High-textured paper is a risk at best, so use a good quality plain stationery stock.

- Be concise, yet use enough key words and phrases to define your skills, experience, education and professional affiliations.

- For on-line help, visit Resumix's site at *http://www.resumix. com/resume_tips.html,* where you'll find tips, a resume builder form, and an excellent example.

Submitting On-Line Resumes

Some on-line job centers allow you to search and apply to several posted openings at the same time, to post your resume for review by human resource personnel and to read job postings from many organizations. Many companies have on-line forms for presenting your resume. Make sure you *read the directions* and *practice* before you send or post yours. Avoid the temptation simply to sit down, identify openings or places to post your resume, fill in the blanks and zap it off. Most of us write from two to twenty-two drafts of our resume before we finally send it off in answer to an opportunity. When filling out an on-line resume form, it is wise to download the form, develop your responses and then enter them on the form. Print and read the form, making sure it represents you well, that all the information is complete and that there are no typos.

Eliminate anything from your resume that may make it unreadable. For example, if you feel that you simply *must* show prospective employers a sample of the custom hats you design, develop a personal Web site and invite interested employers to visit you there. Include your Web site URL as part of your cover letter. Include in your resume key words that describe your marketing skills, hat creation experience, and Web site design. Just do not try to include a graphic of the hat in an on-line resume form.

The Monster Board (*http://www.monster.com*) is one of several on-line job centers. To post your resume for prospective employers to review or to respond to jobs listed in their job bank, you must complete their form. Cut and paste your accomplishment statements and other information into the appropriate places. The following sample will help you decide in advance which information belongs where. *Always* read the directions at the Web site before completing these forms.

COVER LETTERS

An on-line job search has some significant differences from a traditional paper-based job search when it comes to cover letters. Key differences in the on-line cover letter include the following:

- Many on-line resume forms contain space for the cover letter to be an integral part of the document, so you won't create a separate letter. When this option is in the form, be sure to use it. An easy way to complete the cover letter portion is to cut and paste text from a word processed letter you have sent to other prospective employers. The good news: The form blanks let you paste in text from nearly any document. The bad news: Many of these forms do not have a word wrap function, so that unless you enter hard returns at the end of each line, your document will run off the page. **Remember, read the directions first!**

- It will be more difficult to use the "compare experience to requirements" format for your cover letter, which is a very good way of making sure that your qualifications get noticed. The comparison is most often presented in a side-by-side table format. If you are using e-mail or a fill-in-the-blanks form, this will present a challenge. The best way to get around this problem is to use the paragraph header method. The following figure shows a sample cover letter that uses this method.

- Be sure to include a Key Word section in your resume, because the database will be searched and matches made electronically. Read the job description carefully and make sure your letter and resume contain some of those terms and phrases.

But the basic function of the cover letter remains the same:

- A cover letter is a business document that introduces your resume and states the purpose of your communication.

- Your cover letter is a sales tool. Its purpose is to convince a prospective employer that you have qualifications and experience that make you worth interviewing for a job opening.

Lynn Jobseeker · 13344 SW Worry Free Lane · Miles Around, MN 33645

May 31, 1997

Gotrocks Company
P. O. Box 55443
Gotrocks, IL 61834

Attn: Human Resources

I am forwarding my resume for your consideration for the Underwater Basketweaving Division Manager position as posted on your Web site. My skills and experience meet your requirements very well.

You require:

1. Excellent communication skills

2. Supervisory experience

My experience:

1. More than five years developing technical manuals and employee communications such as newsletters, benefits announcements and instructional materials

2. Hands-on supervision of an employee relations department comprised of five HR specialists, three administrative employees and two benefits coordinators

I will be happy to meet with you to discuss my salary requirements and the results I can bring to your Underwater Basketweaving Division.

Sincerely,

L. Jobseeker
lynnj@online.com
333-222-1111

Cover Letter with Paragraph Headers

- Your cover letter may be in answer to an advertised opening (whether posted on a Web site or printed in a newspaper). Or it may be a "cold call," inquiring about possible openings and selling the reader on your potential.

- Cover letters are most effective when they are brief, written in the active voice and compare your qualifications to the requirements of the job. Neatness and correct spelling and grammar do count. Print it, proofread it and have another person proofread it before you send it off.

PERSONAL CYBERCOMMERCIALS

A personal cybercommercial is a concise statement that can be used to describe your experience and accomplishments in about 30 to 40 seconds (about as long as the average listener can stay focused) or can be read in a few seconds. Most of the on-line resume forms ask for such a statement. Develop yours and use it to introduce yourself in your in-person job search. Consider the following example:

My name is Val Rosario. I have ten years of experience with increasing responsibility in sales management. As the leading salesperson for Xanadu Widgets nationally, I established a reputation for accountability and results with my national sales accounts. As a manager, I have developed five sales leaders in the manufacturing equipment industry. My strengths are developing talented people, selling and marketing.

Presenting yourself in a positive way will be even more important during your on-line search campaign than the face-to-face campaign that is going on at the same time. First impressions are lasting and can help you gain consideration from a prospective employer whether nearby or halfway around the globe.

Many people freeze up when someone says, "Tell me about your strengths." They consider it bragging to praise themselves and communicate about their skills in an objective way. In presenting yourself on-line, you must use this opportunity to present your experience, skills and capabilities to a contact person or potential employer.

How could the example below be used to create a favorable impression on-line? (Keep this question in mind as you review some of the on-line tools described later.)

> *My name is Trinidad McGee and I have more than fifteen years of experience in residential property management. I am the Plant Services Manager at Jackpot Commercial Investment Bank, a major employer in the residential lending industry. My areas of expertise lie in construction management, property lease contracts, management and facilities planning.*

 ## Exercise: Creating Your Own Cybercommercial

Develop a "tell me about your strengths" statement using the following format:

> *My name is_____ I have_____ years of experience in _____ . I am (or, most recently I have been) _____ . Before that I _____ . My personal strengths include_____ and _____ . I*

have (developed expertise)(proven capabilities)(become accomplished) in and _____ .

_____

Additionally, I am especially proud of my ability to _____

_____

_____ .

Advanced Marketing

So far, the Internet, with all its growth, is still underused. One study by a major outplacement firm showed that only about 19 percent of 500 candidates interviewed had logged onto the Internet. The research also showed that those who had logged on found an average of five job leads each, and each scored more than one job interview as a result of searching the Internet. Besides posting an on-line resume in response to job listings you find on the Internet, consider these advanced marketing techniques:

- Use a translating service to market yourself in another language. This service is not in real-time (that is, you don't see your words translated as you type), but you will receive your translation via e-mail, usually within a few hours. It isn't perfect, but it is a free service. The URL is *http://www.globalink.com.*

- Market yourself to smaller companies with a direct mailing. By doing key-word searches, tap into databases from various publications to find information about smaller companies. Or search BigYellow *http://www.bigyellow.com,* a database of 16 million companies listed in the yellow pages, for the names and addresses of firms in any area code or zip code, by industry.

■ Market your skills to specific industries. For example, for federal government openings, try starting at *http://www.fedworld.gov*. Insurance professionals can target that market at *http://www.connectyou.com/ins*. If you can think of a job category, there is probably a site for it.

■ Post your resume on the major career-focused Web sites, such as the Monster Board (*http://www.monster.com*), the Online Career Center (*http://www.occ.com*) and in the free classifieds that can be found in most of the sites.

■ Register with on-line directories and classifieds such as Four11 at *http://www.four11.com* and WhoWhere? at *http://www.whowhere.com*, which are directories of e-mail addresses and on-line community identifiers.

BE A BRAND NAME: E-MAIL, SIGNATURES, AND WEB SITES

More than 80 percent of Internet users state that their primary use of the Internet is for e-mail. Even if you're already on-line, you should consider some issues specific to the use of e-mail in a job search.

Configuring Your E-mail Address

Most commercial on-line services and Internet access providers allow you some leeway in deciding how the name portion of your e-mail address can read, but most providers have some restrictions on how a user name can be configured. For example, some require all lowercase letters while others allow a mix of upper- and lowercase; and some limit the number of characters your user name can contain. Here are some examples:

first/last name: *terrysanchez@e-mail.com*
first initial/last name: *tsanchez@e-mail.com*
first name/last initial: *terrys@e-mail.com*
"vanity" or "special interest": *WildOne@e-mail.com,*
  Catlover@e-mail.com

You should ask yourself whether your e-mail address is appropriate and whether it identifies you in a professional way. An e-mail address may be the single most important tool for job searching on the Internet. Why?

- Having an e-mail address on your resume is the equivalent to having a phone number on your resume in the 1940s. It means you have taken a step into the information age that eliminates barriers, no matter what your field, function or level.

- It allows you to monitor the invisible job market via listservs, bulletin boards and chat rooms.

- It reduces the expense of producing and mailing resumes.

- It gets your resume into the hands of recruiters in minutes, not days.

- It suggests you have basic skills for today's workplace— computer literacy and the ability to use an electronic communication medium—which means the employer won't have to spend time training you.

- It expands your networking capabilities. You'll be able to take classes by e-mail, contact former colleagues, communicate with prospective employers anywhere and complete any of a hundred communication tasks more efficiently.

Creating an Electronic Signature

Most e-mail software programs allow you to include electronic signatures automatically at the end of your message. Such signatures become an electronic business card and can include a variety of information. The basic signature includes your real name and your e-mail address (see samples below).

```
                    *

                  * * *

                 * * * * *

 * * * * * * * * * * * * * * * * * * * * * * * *

         * RESOURCES FOR  *   Carrie Straub,

            * SUCCESS     *   Director of StarBuilding

          * * * * * * * * * * * * * * * * *   Portland - Olympia - San Francisco

          * * * * * *        * * * * * * *

           * * * * * *  Providing  * * * * *

         * * * * * Tomorrow's Skills * * * *

        * * * *        Today        * * * *

      * *          503-286-1252        * *

    *  e-mail: carries@us.world.net         *
```

```
O-O-   See http://people.delphi.com/walthowe/
( J )   and the Swash Zone (shelter from the surf)
(  )   at http://www.delphi.com/swashzone/ and my
 ( ))   Learning Center at http://world.std.com/~walthowe/
```

```
  / \__      "Happiness isn't something you experience, it's
 (  @\___       something you remember"
 /       o                               \/\
 / (____/                                ( )
 /____/ U ~~~~~~~~abuys@voicenet.com ```````.( o ).
```

A signature allows the reader to identify you and send you an individual e-mail if he or she wishes. It can also provide other information—for example, your phone number, office location or Web site URL.

Signatures are also a way to be creative and present something unique about yourself. Look at others' signatures and get some ideas. Since each e-mail software package is a little different, start by reading the available documentation for your software.

Some signature Netiquette:

- Keep your signature to a few lines, all created in ASCII text
- Go easy on the graphics, since they can be distracting
- Be creative
- Have fun

Things To Consider

This is a job search—your e-mail address will be used by a prospective employer.

- Do you really want to be addressed as "WildOne" when you are being contacted for an interview?

■ Is your e-mail address easy to spell and type? Difficult words or keyboard combinations may result in typos, which means the e-mail contact gets returned to the sender and a busy manager never asks you to get in touch.

■ Cutesy signatures, like off-beat answering machine messages, are fine for personal situations. While cybersearching, remember to consider what is communicated (beyond the actual content) of your signature.

Sending Resumes or Other Information as Attachments

Your e-mail software will most likely allow you to send a document as an "attachment" along with your message, rather than including the entire document in the body of your e-mail. This is an extremely convenient tool—until you send something created in software that the receiving party doesn't have available, in which case the attachment won't be readable.

In job searching it's safest to assume that the other end does not have the same software. So . . .

■ If you are planning to send a complex document, ask the recipient if he or she can open files created in the program you are using. Be sure to specify the version as well.

■ Enter your resume in a site's on-line form and e-mail a request to clarify the programs in which work samples may be sent.

■ Develop a Web site and post the information you would otherwise send as an attachment. Then you can refer to it in your resume or e-mail.

■ Cut and paste the information into an e-mail. Though you will very possibly lose much of the formatting, many e-mail software programs can accommodate at least basic formats such as italics or bullets.

Creating Your Own Web Site

Most Internet access providers offer space for a personal home page as part of the fee you pay for your connection. The norm is about 5 MB of space, which allows you to present pages of text with links and some graphics—for example, a photo of your most prestigious doghouse design or scanned image of the sales meeting you led.

You can take a class, get lessons from a local user's group, and find information about HTML coding from many sites on-line. You can even download software that allows you to author a Web page at the click of a mouse button—very much like desktop publishing software. However, having the ability to create a Web site is vastly different from being able to create a *successful* one. Spend some time looking at Web sites from a style perspective. There are a lot of sites out there, but how many really look good and are easy to navigate?

Tips for Creating a Professional Web Page

➤ If you plan your personal Web site to be more than one or two pages with a couple of links, it should be mapped or storyboarded before production. (If you know where you're going, you are more likely to know when you get there.)

➤ Keep graphics, backgrounds and fonts as simple as possible.

➤ Cute has no place, unless you are a puppy salesperson or designer of children's clothing. And "cute" often takes extra time to download. Consider whether a prospective employer will wait.

➤ Link your home page to an appropriate industry, association or search engine. For example, if you have no interest in working in Zimbabwe, link your page to the local chapter of a trade organization, not the international one.

➤ Use color to accentuate, not decorate. Same with pictures and animation (they take time to download).

➤ The text needs to be spelled correctly, well written and punctuated appropriately. Claiming excellent written communication skills and presenting a poorly done Web page will do you more harm than good.

➤ Promote your Web page with little or no cost on the many search engines such as Yahoo, Infoseek, AltaVista or Excite. These engines have automated forms.

➤ Consider "banner" marketing: These ads cost about $20—$50 per thousand hits but will direct potential employers to your site. Thunder Lizard at *http://www. thunderlizard.com* specializes in this tactic.

TIPS FOR ORGANIZING YOUR ELECTRONIC TOOLS

1. Create a mail list by cutting and pasting addresses into the automatic addressing feature of your e-mail program. Such a list will help reduce the number of messages that bounce back because of typos.

2. Create an automated list by giving the list a title, for example, "Six-month Resume List," and include on it the names of all the companies to which you will resubmit your resume and cover letter every six months.

3. "Lurking" is a good way to learn how people in a newsgroup communicate before you post to such a list. Select a few places to lurk and read articles for a week before you get active. Then put the address in the automatic addressing feature so that you can get messages done quickly.

4. Go on-line to collect your e-mail, and then go off-line to compose new mail or responses. This is especially important if you are using an on-line service for which you pay by the minute.

5. There is no central listing of e-mail addresses. The most reliable way to get an e-mail address is to call the individual you would like to contact and ask for the address. Alternatively, go to *http:// www.netscape.com/home/internet-white-pages.html* to find search tools that will help you locate e-mail addresses that have been registered.

6. Most viruses attach themselves to programs. Make sure you have a good virus detection program in operation.

7. Set up files by topics, companies or purpose, and sort your e-mail messages frequently. Delete unimportant stuff regularly.

8. Use your password and keep your job search files separate from family or personal files. Attaching your grandmother's last e-mail instead of your resume to a message intended for a prospective employer is uncool—accident or not.

NETIQUETTE GUIDELINES: TIPS FOR SUCCESSFUL CYBERCOMMUNICATING

- Write below your target reader's reading level. The average person in the United States reads at a fifth-grade level. The average professional reads at about the twelfth-grade level.

- Keep paragraphs short and sweet. Keep sentences shorter and sweeter. Be clear, not cryptic.

- White space isn't wasted—it improves both clarity and willingness to read. In the absence of color and formatting (which are absent from ASCII text files), readers are often "turned off" by the density of a written message.

- Choose your words carefully, and construct your sentences well. Think about whether a statement could be mis-interpreted. For example, consider this warning message, which appears on many plastic bags: "To avoid risk of suffocation, keep away from small children." We get the intent, but that's not the literal meaning of the example. In a global communication environment, not everyone has a fine-tuned understanding of language nuances.

- Avoid abbreviations, acronyms and passive voice sentences. (Check out Strunk & White's *The Elements of Style* if you don't know the difference between active and passive voice.)

- Paragraphs are "chunks" of information that are related in some way. People only grasp about seven things at once. So keep your ideas related and grouped.

- Use subject lines carefully. Don't waste your reader's time with misleading subject lines.

- Use a mix of upper- and lowercase; it's much easier to read than all capitals.

- Be careful of the contextual meaning of words. For example, there are 27 definitions for "run," depending on the context.

- Remember that this is an international network. Some people who read your communications may not have an excellent command of your language.

- Spelling, punctuation and grammar are important. Your prospective employer may be on the same listserv you are: Make a good impression every time.

- "Flaming" (making angry or hurtful statements on the Internet) is inappropriate. Bulletin boards, listservs and Usenet newsgroups are places for thoughtful discussion and interaction. Some providers will take away your privileges if you use expletives or bad Netiquette.

- You are responsible for what you write. Proofread and review Internet communications carefully before sending them. Otherwise, you could blow your chances for a job just by sending a document that contains errors or misinformation.

- If you are using your employer's e-mail system to job search, your employer "owns" the e-mail, responses and information and has no obligation to allow you access if you leave or if you have violated company policy in some way. Never offer inside information, violate confidentiality agreements or spread rumors.

SECTION

4

Resources for Your Electronic Job Search

After you've read this section, you should be able to:

- *List some of the job search possibilities available on the Internet*

- *Define the places that you'd like to visit and look them up*

- *Expand the scope of your on-line job search possibilities and integrate your on-line activities with your "in-person" efforts*

Since you're planning to job search and want to market yourself on the Internet, the first thing to do when you get on-line is to take a good look around. Web browser software programs allow you to bookmark or hotlist sites that are of interest so that you can go back there easily. This feature is a key component of your on-line job search.

WHAT'S OUT THERE?

Over the past couple of years, resources on the Internet have multiplied like crazy, as have the available search tools. Many of these tools can be downloaded from the Internet at little or no cost, and many of the larger Internet access providers include browser software and search tools with their service packages. Increasingly, commercial versions of these tools are being marketed that have some additional features. Let your budget and requirements dictate which software you use. These tools give you the power to:

- Post your resume or read posted resumes to get ideas

- Find job postings by searching job databases

- Research employer listings and information, including policies, benefits, locations, products and reputation

- Conduct market research regarding qualifications, industry growth, compensation and more

- Network

- Distribute electronic business cards with every message

- Contact resume posting services whose sites are visited by large employers worldwide

- Read career magazines and get career coaching

- Find and take advantage of educational opportunities

- Establish an e-mail presence and mail your resume without cost of postage or paper

There are many possibilities for conducting your job search over the Internet. The following sections describe some of the Internet marketing tools available both to companies and individuals.

Your Own Domain Name: myname.com

To make your Internet presence stand out among the rest of the candidates, register your own domain name, a pseudonym for the computer that hosts your Internet presence. Most Internet access providers will register your domain name for you. Charges vary, but it should cost less than $200 for a two-year term. You can use your domain name for a Web site address or as part of your e-mail address. A good reason to consider registering your own domain name is that even if you change Internet access providers, your e-mail address remains unchanged. The commercial on-line services such as America Online don't offer this feature.

A Personal Home Page

Home pages are the display documents of the World Wide Web. They are easy to build, but there is only one way to make them available: They must be stored with an Internet access provider. Most providers offer a small personal home page site along with your connection account. More elaborate sites can be expensive, but some "free" sites still exist.

HTML (HyperText Markup Language) is used to create documents to be viewed on the Web, and it is relatively easy to learn and use. The best source of information on HTML is the Internet itself. Many point-and-click authoring tools are available for free or as shareware on the Internet. Tutorials abound. Go to *http://www.ncsa.vivc.edu/General/Internet/WWW/HTMLPrimer.html* for a tutorial on writing HTML documents and links to similar sites.

At GeoCities, you can put up a personal home page on a site that is organized into 18 "neighborhoods" that share common interests. For example, Athens is a neighborhood for teachers and writers. Apply for a free personal home page at *http://www.geocities.com.*

A Web Site for Your Industry or Job Search Group

By creating a site for a group, you can leverage your visibility with employers by including the Web site address on your cover letters, e-mail messages or personal business cards. However, you need to be careful not to confuse busy work with job-searching. If you find that creating such a site distracts you from your core business—job-searching or making a career change—network to find partners who will share the work. Go to *http://cgi.netscape.com* for help getting your site on the Web.

Moderating an E-mail List of Professionals in Your Industry

In listservs, each message is first read by a moderator, who decides if the message is appropriate for the group. If the message meets the guidelines for the group, it is forwarded to everyone on the list. Answers and comments are displayed by the same process. Your list can become a publicly accessible list, and you can invite the employers in your function (manufacturing, human resources and so on) to post jobs there, or you can use it to form a virtual job search network for an industry or locality. Examples of special interest e-mail lists include

■ *Legal issues in cyberspace:* Discussion and information about legal issues in cyberspace. Contact: *listproc-request@counsel.com.* Leave the subject line blank, and type *subscribe cyberspace-law [firstname] [lastname]* in the body of your e-mail message (replacing *[firstname] [lastname]* with your first and last names—or such pseudonyms as you prefer). Consider checking out this site if you are creating your own Web site or plan to moderate a listserv.

■ *Offroad driving:* Discussion of 4 × 4 and off-road driving. Contact: *offroad-request@ai.gtri.gatech.edu.*

■ *Wine:* Discussion about fine wines, making wine and tasting wine. Contact: *majordomo@niagara.com.* Type *subscribe wine* in the body of your e-mail message.

Networking Opportunity Unlimited

Here's an example of the hidden job market at work, a posting from a listserv moderated by a consultant in the Portland OR area. Very well connected in the business community, Eric Wilson's listserv is a place for human resources professionals to gather information about HR issues, announce openings and gather responses from interested professionals. Notice also that his e-mail address contains the name of his company (hrisolutions), his signature line provides his snailmail address as well as an active link to his website.

It may look like a regular, plain-old e-mail . . . but it's opportunity × 5. P.S. Don't apply for this one. . . . the name of the company has been changed!

***************************** XXXØXXX ****************************

Human Resources Benefits Manager

JackPot Mortgage Corporation has an attitude about life and the way we do business. We hire people who like to dig in and find solutions for our clients.

We are looking for someone to manage and administer employee benefits plans for all corporate, branch and subsidiary employees located in 16 different geographic locations. Coordinate benefit data system and give presentations to employees concerning benefits. The position will perform multiple tasks in an environment of changing priorities.

Requires Bachelor's degree in HR Management of Business with three to five years experience in analyzing, evaluation and administering employee benefit programs including retirement benefits, specifically 401(K) plans. Must have substantial experience in managing vendor relationships and interpreting insurance carrier contracts for the administration of employee benefit programs.

If you are interested in being a part of a dynamic team with a nonconforming style and attitude, please contact Wel Spent at 444-4700 X 404 or fax your resume to 444-4444.

****
Eric R. Wilson, President
HR Integrated Solutions, Inc.
PO Box 80337, Portland, Oregon 97280-1337 (USA)
****
E-Mail me at: erwilson@hrisolutions.com
****

The Human Resource Professional's Gateway to the Internet is found at *http://www.hrisolutions.com/*

Earn a "Virtual" Master's Degree

From the Ivy League to local colleges, the number of universities using the Internet to deliver what in the past were called correspondence classes or distance learning has grown phenomenally. Schools offer so-called campus-free degrees that allow students to be linked interactively to instructors. These programs are highly rated, with competitive entrance and accreditation by some of the most prestigious schools in the world. If you have been wondering how to find the time to pursue that degree, you can do it now, on-line in a portable environment. Start at *http://www.marylhurst.edu* to investigate some examples of available on-line courses.

Don't have the money? Check out the Financial Aid Information home page at *http:www.finaid.org/finaid.html,* sponsored by the National Association of Student Financial Administrators.

Lifelong Learning, a college and career consulting group, gives great financial aid information and advice about transferring credits. Try them at *http://homepages.together.net/ ~ lifelong/ adultaid.html* for more information.

INTERNET RESOURCES FOR YOUR JOB SEARCH

Getting familiar with the available resources is the key to an effective cybersearch. Eliminate the intimidation factor by using the tools available. New technologies are coming on-line every day. Now that you've updated your job search toolbox as well as your resume, it's time to start a list of your own special places of interest. Try these on for size:

Career Centers/Job Posting Databases

■ America's Job Bank (*http://www.ajb.dni.us/html/seekers.html*): Cooperative effort between the U.S. Department of Labor and 1,800 state employment service offices; contains more than 100,000 job opportunities primarily in the military and federal government.

■ Business Job Finder at The Ohio State University Web site (*http://www.cob.ohio-state.edu/dept/fin/osujobs.htm*): Easy to find using the Infoseek search engine and putting "Business + Job + Finder" in the search topic box.

■ CareerMosaic (*http://www.careermosaic.com*): The total site; J.O.B.S data base lets you narrow your search using forms, provides a list of jobs that meet your criteria.

■ CareerPath (*http://www.careerpath.com/*): Classified employment listings from six of the country's largest newspapers.

■ CareerSite (*http://www.careersite.com/*): Confidential candidate profiles; other career-related services.

■ E-Span (*http://www.espan.com*): Service that e-mails you job descriptions that match your registered profile; job bank listings available for search.

■ Internet Business Network (*http://interbiz.com*): Listing of top 25 recruiters, with links to data banks dedicated to specific professions.

■ Internet Job Locator (*http://www.joblocator.com/jobs/*): Combines all major job-search engines on one page and lets you do a search of all of them

■ National Business Employment Weekly (*http://nbew.com/*): A good place to start exploring for management and executive jobs.

■ Job Hunt: Meta List (*http://job-hunt.com*): List of resources, divided into special interest categories such as federal employment, industry employment and so on.

■ "Job Resources on the Internet" (Use Gopher to find this comprehensive list of employment opportunities and job search resources under "All Guides" on The Clearing House of Subject-oriented Guides at the University of Michigan)

■ JobTrak (*http://www.jobtrak.com*): Largest on-line job listing service in the United States.

■ Kaplan (*http://www.kaplan.com*): Interviewing practice; personality, work preference and educational testing.

■ The Monster Board (*http://www.monster.com/home.html*): Searchable index of high-tech companies, mostly in the computer industry.

■ Online Career Center (*http://www.occ.com*): Career center and employment data bank.

■ The Riley Guide (*http://www.dbm.com/jobguide*): Includes resources for job listings and other job-related information on the Internet.

Newsgroups

■ For a list of employment-oriented newsgroups, use the Monster Board Newsgroup Search Engine or go the *http://www.shsu.edu/~ org_shacs/jobs-list.html#news*. (Make sure your web browser is configured to use a news server.)

■ Deja News (*http://www.dejanews.com*): career-related news group

■ Global Internet News Agency (*www.gina.com/*)

Employer Listings and Information

■ Search for the specific company in which you are interested, and then read about the company's policies, benefits, locations, products and reputation. You can first try inserting the company name into the general format for a URL (*http://www.companyname.com*). If that doesn't work, go to *http://www.w100.com*, which is a Web directory featuring links to 100 major company Web sites. Or try *http://www. companiesonline.com/* which provides a searchable, linked listing of companies who are online. Still no luck? Try one of the search engines such as Infoseek or Yahoo and select the "Business" button.

■ Search in BigYellow (*http://www.bigyellow.com*) for all the companies in your area code under a specific industry, and then use a search engine to locate the company's home page.

■ The Internet Job Locator (*http://www.joblocator.com/jobs/*) combines all major job-search engines on one page and lets you search all of them.

■ Watch for print ads from the organization or company in which you are interested. These ads often include URLs for company Web sites.

Resources for Market Research

■ Salary Survey from Jobsmart: *http://jobsmart.org* or at Abbott Langer Management Consultants at *http://www. abbott-langer.com/*.

■ U.S. Department of Labor's Occupational Outlook Handbook can be found by going to *http://www.dol.gov*, clicking on the Search function button and entering "Occupational Outlook Handbook" in the topic box. Provides data and

projections about salaries, growth potential, job requirements and educational requirements for careers, industries
and job families.

■ First Virtual (*http://www.firstvirtual.com*): Home page of a
company that purports to be the creator of the Internet
Payment System, which makes it possible for people to
buy and sell information over the Internet.

■ World Lecture Hall (*http://www.utexas.edu/world/lecture/
index.html*) a list of links to pages of on-line class delivery
from all over the world.

■ Small Business Administration: The SBA home page (*http:/
/www.sbaonline.sba.gov/*) helps you find the resources you
need to start and expand a business. Menus help you
access information, training, shareware applications, data
from other federal agencies and links to other resources.

■ "Push" technology: New technology that allows you to
select sites that interest you and automatically updates
you when changes are made to the information on the
site. Visit *http://www.intermind.com* for a rundown on how
this technology works. Pointcast (*http://www.pointcast.com*)
is one of the providers of this type of technology.

■ The Excite search engine (*http://www.excite.com*) features
"City Maps," which will help you find available resources
in most U.S. cities. Use these resources to find information
about the area in which you are job-seeking or to find the
home page of the city or state where you want to relocate.

On-line Classifieds

If you are one of those job searchers who has great luck getting
employed by responding to the classifieds, this category is for
you. More and more newspapers have put their classifieds on-
line. The Job Hunt Meta List (*http://www.job-hunt.org*) has a

"classified ads" category which takes you to a site (*http://www.careerpath.com*) and lets you search the classifieds of over 30 newspapers including *The Boston Globe; Chicago Tribune; Los Angeles Times; The New York Times; San Jose Mercury News; The Washington Post; The Seattle Times; The Sacramento Bee; The Miami Herald;* and the *Denver Post.*

On-line Services for Special Populations

You can tap into an amazing number of Web sites, listservs, bulletin boards and chat rooms that are targeted for specific industries, populations and skills. Some examples of special interest sites and resources:

Executive Recruiters

Exec-U-Net (*http://www.execunet.com*): A nationwide networking and career management organization for senior-level executives and professionals, listing unadvertised openings at $75,000 and up by individual membership only. Positions cover general management, finance, human resources, operations, engineering, sales, marketing, consulting and legal.

Washington State Executive Search Service (*http://www.wa.gov/dopless.html*): A state agency which recruits for executive-level positions in the Pacific Northwest.

Resources for Minorities

Saludas Web (*http://saludas.com*): A site devoted to promoting Hispanic careers and education, supported by Saludos Hispanos Magazine.

The Black Collegian (*http:/www.blackcollegian.com/*): This career and self-development site is the electronic version of *The Black Collegian* magazine, sponsored by those who support its mission to provide career development for people of color.

Women's Resource Lists:

Global Fund for Women Links (*http://www.igc.apc.org/gfw/*): This page includes links to the following resources:

- CareerMosaic's Diversity Links for Women and Minorities (*http://www.careermosiac.com*)

- wwwomen: Links to women's sites/resources (*http://www.wwwomen.com/*)

- Advancing Women (*http://www.advancingwomen.com*)

- South Asian Women's Net (*http://www.gunung.com/seasiaweb/*)

- American Society of Women Entrepreneurs (*http://women.aswe.org/aswe/*)

- Women-Connect-Asia (*http://women-connect-asia.com*)

- Global Fund for Women (*http://www.igc.apc.org/gfw/*)

- Women's Web (*http://womweb.com*)

- Women's Wire (*http://www.women.com/guide/*)

- Yahoo's Women's Public Interest Groups
  and Women's Studies
  (*http://www.yahoo.com* (search on "women")

Nonprofit Organizations and Cultural Resources:

- American Studies
  (*http://www.wcsu.ctstate.edu/sarp/americanstudies.html*)

- John December's Earth Science and Environmental Listings
  (*http://www.vmedia.com/books/wwww_2nd/sec4/subsec5/
  list12.html*)

- KFAI's Community Links: music and culture
  (*http://www.mtn.org/internet/orgs.html#music*)

- Envirolink's Mailing List of Organizations
  (*http://manatee.envirolink.org/archives/*)

- Legal Resources on the Internet
  (*http://www.laws.com/legal_resource.html*)

- Go Organic
  (*http://www.go-organic.com*)

Academics, librarians, software developers, cat breeders and wine growers . . . a little searching will provide more links than you can pursue. By using a search engine such as Infoseek or Excite, you can count on finding references to any facet of a particular industry or topic. There are many others, too numerous for anyone but the Internet Yellow Pages to list.

Electronic Job Fairs

These "virtual job fairs" allow you to post your resume at a site that will be reviewed by recruiters for industry or functional areas. Try the Monster Board, (*http://www.monster.com*) and select the "Job Fairs" button.

Using the Library in Your Search

In addition to providing terminals and Internet connections, libraries are treasure troves for job seekers. Examples of services they offer by remote access (ie, you can gain access to these on-line resources from your home computer):

- Automated catalog of library holdings which can be searched by title or subject key words, author
- Community events calendar
- Community organizations database that can be searched by name, subject, any word or any number
- Dictionaries
- Databases held by local academic libraries which contain indexes to journal articles and other networked resources

Call your local library and ask for a brochure about their on-line services, what classes they offer, and the phone number for dial-up connection. Find out if they have a home page.

Net censors

Net censors allow you to block access to specific Internet sites. Job searching can take you to many sites, so if you are concerned about others access to the Internet, you may want to consider purchasing censoring software. Some use lists they compile, others search for prohibited terms. Here are a couple of examples:

- SafeSurf Internet Rating System (*http://www.safesurf.com*)
- A long list of software can also be found at *http://ipw. internet.com/censoring/index.html.*

Reminders for Success

Now that you have increased your skill in using the resources available in Cyberspace, remember to:

1. Create a personal business card that has your e-mail address on it.

2. Initiate at least one new search or contact a week.

3. Go to your local library and find out what resources they have available to support your jobsearch.net.

4. Visit your local employment security office and check their offerings.

5. Develop a bookmarked list of job search resources that pertain to your search.

6. Update your list of bookmarks at least monthly.

7. Talk about it. Knowing the lingo, sharing discoveries, helping others with their searches will expand your network and increase your confidence.

8. Get your resume ready for cybersearch transmitting.

9. Share your skills with another job seeker. (You haven't really learned a new skill until you've taught it.)

10. Put it on your resume as a skill or qualification: "Use the Internet to define and research resources."

APPENDIX

A

Internet
Basics

To use the Internet, you must have access to a personal computer that can communicate with other computers connected to the Internet. Computers communicate with each other by modems connected to phone lines or to special data lines. Though many have tried, no one has yet successfully "mapped" the Internet. A very simple picture of a connection to the Internet would look something like the figure below. Remember that this arrangement is constantly changing, growing and being "tweaked" by new services. It is truly the new frontier.

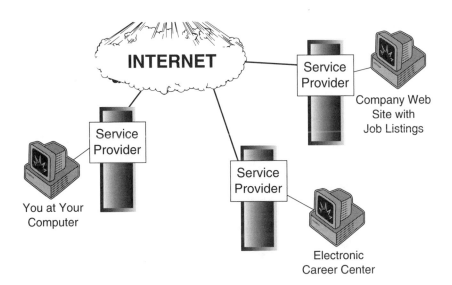

Part 1: HOW DOES THE INTERNET DO WHAT IT DOES?

To market your skills on the Internet, you need a very basic understanding of how the Internet operates. Though no one "manages" the Internet, some technologies provide the foundation to it. Two of these technologies are *client/server* and *hypertext/hypermedia.*

Client/Server

In its simplest term, a *client* requests information, and the *server* supplies it. Computer systems connected to the Internet—whether part of a local area network (LAN) in a company or a single machine in your spare bedroom—use a client/server relationship. A client is a software program running on your computer that is used specifically to ask for information from other computers on the Internet. The computer that supplies the data to the client is called the *server.* (Most computers can be *servers* if they have the appropriate software.) Every computer connected to the Internet has a unique address that is used whenever information is sent or received. Internet addresses usually take the following form:

userid@hostcomputer.subdomain.domain

1. The *userid* refers to the Internet account holder. It is the identifying name you use when you log on to the computer that has your Internet account. Your userid is created when your account is set up. Since this is *not* your password and you *will* be giving it out to people who need to contact you, your personal userid should include at least some part of your first and/or last name (see Section 3 for more on choosing an e-mail name).

2. The *hostcomputer* in your address is most frequently an individual machine located at a particular place. You may or may not have a host name, depending on the type of Internet account you use.

3. A *subdomain* is a group of hosts or local networks that are grouped into larger domains, much like the groups of county governments that comprise a state.

4. The last part of the Internet address represents the largest domain. Today, there are six domains in the United States:

   .com = commercial

   .edu = educational

   .gov = government

   .mil = military

   .net = network

   .org = organization

Other countries have different ways of organizing domain names. So if the address doesn't end in one of these six domains, chances are it's from a country other than the United States (eg, ca for Canada, au for Australia, no for Norway).

Hypertext/Hypermedia

Hypertext is text that contains connections (called *links*) to other text. *Hypermedia* is hypertext with graphics (pictures, sound or video). The *World Wide Web* structures everything that's available on the Internet in an easy-to-use system. To access the Web, you will use Web client software, or a *browser,* such as Mosaic, Netscape, or Microsoft Internet Explorer. Early versions of Netscape are shareware (though a proprietary version is available). Mosaic is provided free of charge from the National

Center for Supercomputing Applications. Microsoft Internet Explorer is a proprietary product of the Microsoft Corporation and is freely available. Web documents are written in a special format called HTML (which stands for HyperText Markup Language).

When you ask your computer to retrieve a document from a server, your Web browser retrieves it, scans it and formats it according to the HTML tags in the text. An interesting sidelight here: The same document can look very different on two separate systems, depending on the options each user sets up and the browser he or she uses.

The location of nearly any resource on the Internet can be determined by a Uniform Resource Locator (URL; pronounced *you-are-el*). If the address of the resource you are looking for starts with *http://www*, the site or document is on the World Wide Web and is a hypertext document. The *http* in a Web address tells the client/server that the information is to be in the *hypertext transfer protocol* format. (The designer of a hypertext document decides which documents will be linked, which text will contain links, and where those links will be directed.) As you become familiar with the addressing protocols, you will begin to find that you can tell a lot about the company just from their URL. The following URL is the address for the Web page of a small company that rebuilds automotive engines: *http://www.aluminumheads.com*.

Based on a graphical user interface and hypertext documents, the Web is capable of handling multimedia. The key word here is multimedia: This combination of graphics, animation, music, text, speech and video via hypertext links has increased the glitz of the Internet.

Part 2: GETTING CONNECTED

You'll need to shop around a bit to find the best way to access the Internet. Pricing for access has leveled out after a period when the cost of access varied wildly. Local providers offer connections through a local telephone number, so phone charges generally don't apply. Many companies offer service that allows you to connect to an 800 number from anywhere in the United States.

Internet access providers offer connections to the Internet from servers that are connected by dedicated phone lines. These access providers come in a variety of levels and price ranges. Some have direct connections (they own the servers and the phone lines); others rent server space from large network providers.

You don't need to own a computer to have access. Many copy centers have computers connected to the Internet, which are available for an hourly fee. There are even cybercafes that offer connection to the Internet on a pay-per-minute basis. Copy centers and cybercafes can be great for browsing the Web, but you can't use these connections for e-mail, and as Section 3 explains, some of the most valuable job-search resources are based on e-mail.

Another option for Internet access is the public library. Some libraries have dedicated terminals and staff who can coach you in getting on line. Check with your main library and local branches.

Assuming that you want full access to the Internet, you'll need to consider the following elements:

- Computer hardware and software
- Modem
- Internet access options
- Internet security
- Advanced Internet features

Computer Hardware and Software

Depending on the type of Internet access you seek, your current computer system may be adequate or you may need to upgrade your system's memory or the size of your hard disk. Your Internet access provider will have some ideas about which types of equipment they are prepared to support. You'll also need to find out from your provider the "minimum system requirements" for the software it gives its subscribers.

You'll need a Web browser and e-mail software. Most Internet access providers supply both of these. The two most common browsers are Netscape and Microsoft Internet Explorer. Some common e-mail software are Eudora, cc:mail, and Claris. Commercial on-line services such as CompuServe and America Online have e-mail and browser capabilities built into their systems.

Go to your local bookstore. Some books about the Internet and search tools include the software you will need or URLs for Web sites where you can download search tools at no cost, assuming you're already connected.

Modem

A modem serves as a "translator" so that your computer (which speaks *digital*) can talk to the phone lines (which speak *analog*). The speed at which your modem can translate is a critical factor in your Internet use. The much-touted graphics, downloading accessibility, and so on are affected by your modem's speed or bps (bits-per-second) of your modem.

If you have a modem that operates at less than 28,800 bps (or 28.8 kbps), you should be prepared for long delays while you're on line, especially if you want to download free software, look at graphics on Web sites, or view multimedia. Prepare for tomorrow when you make this investment: A 28.8 kbps will support your Internet activities much better with only a slightly higher initial outlay. The price of a middle-of-the-line 28.8 kbps modem should be around $100 to $150 for a standard external modem. Internal modems are somewhat cheaper, but if you're planning to access the Internet from more than one computer system (eg, a desktop and a laptop), you won't be able to use one internal modem on both machines.

Getting a second phone line is important, especially if you expect to be on line for any length of time. If you're in the middle of a job search, you don't want your phone line to be tied up a good portion of the day while you're on the Internet.

Internet Access Options

- *Connect through your employer or school.* Most colleges and universities offer free Internet access to their faculty, staff and students, and many government and business offices now have access as part of their LAN or e-mail systems. In many cases, individuals can use their school's or employer's Internet connection, even from their home computer. Remember that you may be posting your resume to a site where your employer is recruiting. (This may be true whether or not you use their connection.) Each site is different, so read the fine print to check for ways to keep your resume out of your employer's database if you don't want them to know you're looking. Also, if you use your company e-mail to send resumes to the competition, beware that the destinations for e-mails and Internet searches may be tracked or reviewed.

- *Connect through a dial-up Internet access provider (ie; a local Internet access provider).* Dial-up accounts are direct Internet connections. Your ability to use a point-and-click user interface will be determined by the specific software you use. Downloaded files come directly to your computer and can be stored in a variety of software platform configurations; retrieval speed will be affected by your modem and browser software.

- *Connect through one of the commercial on-line services (for example, America Online, CompuServe, Prodigy).* Most of the commercial on-line services package their Internet access along with other features that you may or may not need (such as newsreaders, games and stock market tracking). If you already use one of these services, you may want to use the service's Internet connection. Hourly charges made them prohibitive in the past, but most now offer flat-fee access. You may experience difficulty getting on line because of the high ratio of users to modems.

■ *Connect through a shell account.* The Yugo of connections—from your computer to a remote Internet site, shell accounts allow you to send and receive e-mail, participate in discussion groups and retrieve files and other data. They also force you to use the command-line interface to the Internet, downloading is a two-step process and it may be slow and unreliable. Very few providers offer this type of connection.

For the individual job searcher, the choice is usually between a commercial on-line service and a local Internet access provider. This is an area where prices can vary dramatically, based on your real or perceived requirements. If you can use the extras, the on-line services may be for you. Several of the on-line services have a "free" introductory offer that has been packaged with computer magazines or mailed to thousands. Most have 800 numbers. The quality of these services has been hotly debated. Your best bet is to talk to friends or coworkers to see who is using what. Check at your local library for back issues of computer magazines and read up on the different services.

Price is a poor way to judge your connection. Since early 1997, most on-line services have charged a flat fee for service. Unfortunately, the result has been to put new users into competition with millions of other subscribers, causing slow access, system "crashes" and so on. Service and support are the key elements in the equation. Ask questions and compare answers:

■ What are the hours for access to technical support?
■ Do they furnish start-up software?
■ What modems and operating systems do they support?
■ What is the ratio of users to modems?
■ Do they provide space for a personal home page?

- What is the longest their service has been "down" in the past year?
- Do they have more than one connection to the Internet?

Internet Security

Much has been written about the Internet, including stories about government surveillance, hackers, pornography, viruses, and electronic scams. As with any "frontier," the potential for all kinds of inappropriate use is real. However, with appropriate caution—for example, not sending your credit card number to anyone unless you initiated the contact to make a purchase electronically, using virus detection software, or simply not visiting some sites if they offend you—there is every reason to believe that the Internet is less dangerous to you than driving home from work or giving your business card to a new acquaintance at a networking opportunity.

Digital cash and secure transactions, encryption, and privacy of information are critical to the Internet's future. In most cases, you will get a warning notice if information you are sending could be accessed, even for a few seconds.

Privacy is probably more of an issue than is security. Recently an individual purchased driving record information obtained from the Oregon Department of Motor Vehicles and posted it on the Internet. The resulting outcry from the public convinced authorities to review their policies. Encryption (coding) messages to ensure privacy is the topic of several on-line resource databases.

PART 3: ADVANCED INTERNET FEATURES

Job searchers have four primary ways to get or send information by the Internet: e-mail, Usenet newsgroups, listservs, and IRC. The latter three are e-mail-based resources. Other features such as Gopher and FTP enable users to find and download useful information from the Internet.

E-mail

The most commonly used capability of the Internet, the exchange of electronic messages (e-mail) allows almost instantaneous communication. The basic functions of any e-mail program are to send, receive and file or store messages using the computer and phone lines instead of paper and mail service. E-mail messages are transmitted as ASCII (American Standard Character Indicator Integer) text files. These files can be read by almost any program, but generally, most of the formatting features of standard word processing programs (such as italic or boldface) cannot be used. Some formatting is possible with newer versions of e-mail software, but not everyone has or uses the newest versions. This is important to keep in mind when you're creating a resume to be submitted electronically (see Section 3). In this case, the simpler, the better.

Usenet Newsgroups

This worldwide bulletin board system is made up of e-mail messages, programs used to gather up the messages and forward them from machine to machine, and programs that let people read the messages. Groupings of Usenet messages are called *newsgroups*. Accessible by the Internet, newsgroups contain vast storehouses of information on almost every topic imaginable. Think of them as a worldwide collection of automatically updated electronic bulletin boards. Newsgroups include job listings, places where resumes can be posted and places to obtain information about prospective employers.

You subscribe to newsgroups by keying the e-mail address and keying "subscribe" in the subject area. If you later find the list is not helpful to you, key "unsubscribe" in the subject area.

Examples of newsgroups include: *news.newusers.questions* (a newsgroup with questions and answers for users new to the Usenet) and *news.misc.jobs.offered.entry* (a newsgroup offering job listings only for entry-level positions.

Listservs

Listservs are a sort of e-mail party line, usually run by one person or an organization with a specific area of interest. Those with an interest in a topic can e-mail the list and key "subscribe" in the subject area. After that, messages posted by anyone in the listserv group are forwarded, through e-mail, to all subscribers. Job seekers can use listservs to network with professionals and sometimes to find job openings before they are advertised or to learn more about occupations they are exploring. These are excellent sources for tapping into collective wisdom about virtually any topic, and they are frequently the source of job postings that don't appear as ads. They can help you tap into the "invisible" job market. As with newsgroups, you can e-mail a listserv and key "unsubscribe" in the message area to stop receiving messages.

For a list of publicly available mail lists, go to *http://www. NeoSoft.com/internet/paml/indexes.html.*

IRC

Internet Relay Chat (IRC) is a system that enables Internet users to talk in "real time" rather than after a delay, as with e-mail messages. IRC software is available free from the Internet.

Gopher

One of several programs used to search the Internet databases for information, Gopher creates a uniform menu that transfers files, changes directories, contacts and logs into Internet sites for you. It provides relatively easy-to-navigate menus that can be browsed by using the arrow key. Gopher is used to find information on computers designated as *gopher servers* world-wide. Many job listings are available by gopher. Gopher applications search files by their title. Many job-listing databases store their information on gopher servers because they can store and manage large files.

To access a gopher site, you need to be connected to an Internet Service Provider which has a "gopher server," have gopher software and be somewhat experienced in search methods.

FTP

FTP (*file transfer protocol*) is another type of software that is used for transferring large files such as applications. If you download a shareware copy of Web browser software, chances are you will be using the FTP mode, as it is especially for-mulated to transfer large data files quickly. FTP addresses are also URLs but have a slightly different format. An example of an FTP address is *ftp://rtfm.mit.edu/pub/* (the address for a directory of downloadable files located at MIT).

APPENDIX

B

Job Search
Vocabulary

Speaking the language of your industry or job function is very important; however, as you start your cybersearch, you will learn a whole new vocabulary based on the terms you will see used on line. Some key Internet terms are listed below along with some on-line job search buzzwords and acronyms you will find in the ads. At *http://www.paradesa.com* you'll find a complete Internet glossary that is updated regularly. Print yourself a copy.

ASCII text: Basic text files that allow only the use of standard keyboard characters in upper and lower case. Most e-mail programs use ASCII as a standard because it can be used by any type of computer. ASCII text resumes are an important part of any on-line job search.

Applicant Tracking Systems: Computer-based systems that organizations use to compile information about applicants. These systems scan, read, organize, store and retrieve resumes on demand. They may also allow candidates to confirm that their resume or application has been entered into the database and may generate a response to applicants to confirm receipt.

BBS (bulletin board system): A system that lets users connect to a specific computer where they may exchange information, files and discussion comments.

Database: A structured archive of related information, such as a computerized file of job postings that can be searched or a compilation of resumes stored for employers to search.

Freenet: A bulletin board system that provides free community information such as current events and school calendars. Many offer free access to the Internet including e-mail capability.

Key Words: Specific industry, job component, skill or functional terms by which an employer may search a database. Example key words are database management, teamwork, materials control, cash flow analysis, creative design and continuous process improvement.

Key Word Resume: A resume that includes a category specifically for key words, making it easier for a computer search to read the information and find matching qualifications.

Kiosk: Commonly used for retail directories or interactive information presentation, employment kiosks present job seekers with information or on-screen applications to complete.

On-line Help Wanted Ads: Classified employment ads that can be accessed by computer at any time. Examples are on-line ads at the *San Jose Mercury News,* the *Wall Street Journal,* or *Today's Careers* Web site at *http://www.todays-careers.com.* In addition, some services provide job seekers with subscriptions to job ads in specific occupations in any area of the country. For example, E-span (*http://www.espan.com*) will mail you eight matching job descriptions every week once you register.

Resume Database Service: Firms that register candidates in their databases and permit employers to draw from their databases when recruiting to fill openings. Fees for service vary;

listings may target specific geographic regions, industries or skills.

READING THE POSTINGS

Common abbreviations you should know about when reading on-line postings.

AA/EOE = Affirmative Action/Equal Opportunity Employer

BA   = Bachelor of Arts

BS   = Bachelor of Science

BSBA   = Bachelor of Science in Business Administration

CNE   = Certified Network Engineer

JD   = Doctor of Law

DOD   = Department of Defense

DOE   = Department of Energy

MBA   = Master of Business Administration

MS   = Master of Science

M/F/D/V = male/female/disabled/veteran

List others that you find in the job postings you read:

_____

_____

_____

_____

_____

Bibliography

_____ *Looking for Work in All the Right Places*, AARP Bulletin, May 1997

_____ *Predictions on Career Transition Issues*, HR Fact Finder, February 1996

_____ "Web Watchdogs," The Oregonian, May 6, 1997

Bock, Wally. *Getting on the Information Superhighway.* Menlo Park, Calif.: Crisp Publications, 1996

Brame, Gloria. "Seismic Shifts in the Workplace," *Working Woman,* June 1996

Dobrzynski, Judith. "The New Jobs: A Growing Number Are Good Ones," *New York Times*, July 21, 1996

Grusky, Scott. "Winning Resume," *Internet World*, February 1996

Harris, Kellee. "Business on the Web: BluePrint for Business Success," *Journal of Commerce,* July 26, 1996

Mannix, Margaret. "The Home Page Help-Wanteds," *US News & World Report,* October 30, 1995

MaranGraphics. *Internet and the World Wide Web Simplified.* Foster City, Calif.: IDG Books, 1996

Memon, Farham. "Help Wanted Signs Dot Cyberspace," *Interactive Week*, September 16, 1996

Nelson, Anne V. "Cyberbuzz: On-line Job Postings Aren't Just for Techies," *Working Woman,* September 1996

Phillips, Vicki. "Earning a Masters, Virtually," *Internet World*, September 1996

Siwolop, Sana. "Finding a Paycheck On Line," *The New York Times*, January 7, 1996

Tretter, Marietta. *How to Use the Internet.* Emeryville, Calif.: ZD Press, 1996

Toyer, Kathryn. "Internet E-mail," *Women in Business*, September/October, 1996

Wiggans, Richard. "How The Internet Works," *Internet World,* October 1996

On-line resources:

Best of the Links, available at *http://www.cobb.com/int/links.htm*

Netscape Handbook, available at *http://www.netscape.com*

Posting Your Resume on the Internet, Jeff Taylor, available at The Monster Board, *http://www.monster.com*